THE IDEA OF SINGAPORE

SMALLNESS UNCONSTRAINED

IPS-NATHAN LECTURES

THE IDEA OF SINGAPORE

SMALLNESS UNCONSTRAINED

TAN TAI YONG

Published by

World Scientific Publishing Co. Pte. Ltd.

5 Toh Tuck Link, Singapore 596224

USA office: 27 Warren Street, Suite 401-402, Hackensack, NJ 07601

UK office: 57 Shelton Street, Covent Garden, London WC2H 9HE

British Library Cataloguing-in-Publication Data
A catalogue record for this book is available from the British Library.

IPS-Nathan Lecture Series
THE IDEA OF SINGAPORE
Smallness Unconstrained

ISBN 978-981-121-334-2
ISBN 978-981-121-381-6 (pbk)

For any available supplementary material, please visit
https://www.worldscientific.com/worldscibooks/10.1142/11640#t=suppl

Desk Editor: Sandhya Venkatesh

Printed in Singapore

THE S R NATHAN FELLOWSHIP FOR THE STUDY OF SINGAPORE

AND THE IPS-NATHAN LECTURE SERIES

The S R Nathan Fellowship for the Study of Singapore was established by the Institute of Policy Studies (IPS) in 2013 to support research on public policy and governance issues. With the generous contributions of individual and corporate donors, and a matching government grant, IPS raised around S$5.9 million to endow the Fellowship.

Each S R Nathan Fellow, appointed under the Fellowship, delivers a series of IPS-Nathan Lectures during his or her term. These public lectures aim to promote public understanding and discourse on issues of critical national interest.

The Fellowship is named after Singapore's sixth and longest-serving President, the late S R Nathan, in recognition of his lifetime of service to Singapore.

Other books in the IPS-Nathan Lecture series:

The Ocean in a Drop — Singapore: The Next Fifty Years
by Ho Kwon Ping

Dealing with an Ambiguous World
by Bilahari Kausikan

The Challenges of Governance in a Complex World
by Peter Ho

Can Singapore Fall? Making the Future for Singapore
by Lim Siong Guan

Seeking a Better Urban Future
by Cheong Koon Hean

CONTENTS

FOREWORD

The story of Singapore did not start in 1965; it had been unfolding for centuries prior. The island evolved from a 14th century port polity and regional emporium to a major imperial port city, eventually becoming the sovereign city-state that it is today. During some periods in its history, it existed as an autonomous entity; at other times, it was part of local sultanates, and regional and global empires. The nation state of Singapore is but the latest iteration in a long and varied journey.

A number of underlying themes have informed the plot of this saga. The first is geography. Singapore bears testimony to the dictum that "geography is destiny". Throughout its history, the functions, fortunes and fate of Singapore have been determined by its location at the critical maritime intersection in Southeast Asia and the meeting point between two oceans. Location has been exploited, time and again, to emphasise Singapore's inherent advantages for trade and strategic connectivity. Modern Singapore's establishment in the 19th century had very much to do with the utility it held as a strategic location for trade. The port was what brought fame and development to the city thereafter. Its location and character as a maritime city also meant that it had a varied and often amorphous and expandable hinterland. A leitmotif in Singapore's history has therefore been the search for a hinterland.

The primacy of location meant that the fortunes of Singapore were inevitably susceptible to economic developments beyond its shores. Upon independence and the loss of its Malayan hinterland, and given the projected decreasing demand for its entrepôt services, Singapore turned from the regional trade of goods to embed itself in the international market, building tighter communication links and more seamless transport networks.[1] Today, Singapore remains one of the world's most trade-dependent nations, and continues to seek new ways to stay relevant and connected to the rest of the world.

Second, as a nodal point for major trade networks, Singapore was made and remade by the people, goods and ideas that flowed through the island. It has been described as a "child of the diaspora",[2] with diversity and cosmopolitanism being the defining characteristics of the port city. People from all around the world still come to seek investment and work opportunities, and a better life for themselves. Migrants have brought opportunities, dynamism and cultural diversity, even as tensions between foreign and local-born have increasingly had to be navigated.

Third, while physical smallness is a fact for Singapore, the footprints of this tiny island have often been enlarged by its ambition and reach. Singapore was, at its core, a port city, and throughout its history did not really depart from the fundamental instinct to be connected. In the 14th century, Singapore thrived as a regional port. While it remained a secondary feeder port to the Melaka and Johor sultanates from the 15th to 17th centuries, it was able to participate in the growing ecology of trade driven by Chinese and European interests. Colonial Singapore was enlarged

---

[1] S Rajaratnam, "Text of Address Titled 'Singapore: Global City', by Mr S Rajaratnam, Minister for Foreign Affairs, to the Singapore Press Club on February 6, 1972." National Archives of Singapore, 6 February 1972, http://www.nas. gov.sg/archivesonline/data/pdfdoc/PressR19720206a.pdf; National Archives of Singapore, "Connecting Singapore To The World — From Submarine Cables to Satellite Earth Stations," Policy History @ ArchivesOnline, June 24, 2016, http://www.nas. gov.sg/archivesonline/policy_history/connecting-singapore-to-the-world.

[2] T. N. Harper, "Globalism and the Pursuit of Authenticity: The Making of a Diasporic Public Sphere in Singapore," *Sojourn: Journal of Social Issues in Southeast Asia* 12, no. 2 (1997), 261.

by being part of the British eastern empire. Openness and connectivity have made Singapore much more than an island entity of some seven hundred square kilometres. Smallness has never constrained Singapore's ambitions, purpose and significance. This, in my view, is the *idea* of Singapore — an essence and spirit that animates Singapore's evolution throughout its history.

Singapore is a forward-looking country and indeed owes its current success to foresight and planning. Within a short space of time since independence in 1965, the city-state has undergone fundamental and dramatic transformations. The rapid changes in physical and social environments have, however, brought about a disconnect with history. For a future-oriented country, why should we be bothered to know history? It is because understanding the past is not separate from a commitment to the future. An awareness of the continuities and potential disruptions in the journey — and history is replete with these examples — may give us the confidence to negotiate the way ahead. As Yuval Noah Harari, author of the best-selling *Sapiens, A History of Humankind*, reminds us, the study of history enables us to "notice possibilities that our ancestors could not imagine…." It "will not tell us what to choose," but knowing it "at least gives us more options."[3] Ultimately, I hope to stimulate thinking about our past, and what history can show us as we face the present and ponder the future. Here, two things stand out.

First, Singapore's history was not teleological. It had many ups and downs, and unexpected twists. It was characterised by both continuities and disruptions, largely determined by major regional and international changes. Trading patterns, the rise and decline of regional powers, globalisation of commerce, and migrations have had a profound impact on Singapore's historical evolution. These factors will continue to determine Singapore's present and future. Independent Singapore's founding prime minister, Lee Kuan Yew, had wondered what sort of future would await the

---

[3] Yuval Noah Harari, *Homo Deus: A Brief History of Tomorrow* (London: Vintage, 2016), 59.

city-state of Singapore, acknowledging that history had never been kind to small city-states.[4] Singapore cannot take its current success as a small nation state as pre-ordained.

Second, Singapore's identity is a continual work in progress. It cannot be immutable because Singapore is not a civilisational nation with a common culture based on a homogeneous history stretching back thousands of years. Singapore was shaped by movements and shifts, such as adaptation by individuals, families and communities who journeyed to and settled in Singapore in the 1900s when it was a thriving colonial port city. But, Singapore is not simply a product of colonialism. In many ways, colonialism was built upon a pre-colonial past. We need to examine these complex layers of history. We cannot simply define ourselves in the present; our identities are made by our past.

The IPS-Nathan Lectures have provided me with the opportunity to elucidate these enduring themes of Singapore's long history — geography (how location shapes our history), networks (how Singapore was defined by the flows and interactions of people and ideas), globalisation (how Singapore was and will continue to be shaped by the forces of globalism), and the continuous search for identity as a nation state that needs to be a global city. These themes constitute the core arguments of the chapters in this volume.

I hope, through my lectures and the publication of this volume, to contribute to an ongoing conversation about our history. I use the word "conversation" advisedly. The lectures are not meant to be an academic course on the history of Singapore. I will not be describing *what* you should know of our history; if I succeed, these lectures may perhaps suggest *how* we could think of our history.

I am deeply honoured to be the 6th S R Nathan Fellow, and am especially thrilled to be holding a fellowship carrying the name of Mr S R Nathan, a man with a great sense of history. I have had the benefit of spending many hours recording his oral history and have been captivated

---

[4] Lee Kuan Yew, *From Third World to First — The Singapore Story: 1965–2000,* 2nd ed. (Singapore: Marshall Cavendish Editions and Straits Times Press, 2014).

by the stories of his personal and professional life, and the different parts he had played in the more recent chapters of the Singapore story.

I have many people to thank for making these lectures possible. First, I wish to express my gratitude to Janadas Devan, Director, Institute of Policy Studies, for giving me the opportunity as well as providing the stimulation and encouragement for me to share my thoughts on the history of Singapore. He egged me on to do a series of six lectures. It was not an easy undertaking, but I am glad I succumbed to his pressure. I am also grateful for the support of Ariel Tan, Associate Director at the Institute of Policy Studies, for the steady hand with which she managed the lectures from early publicity to the publication of this volume.

I have received very significant support in the research and writing of the lectures and chapters from Tan Li Jen and Rachel Hau, two outstanding research associates who have worked long hours to organise research materials and get my lectures into shape. Their research and intellectual engagement have been instrumental in shaping my thoughts. I thank them also for their patience with my constant last-minute demands.

A special word of appreciation to Kelly Lau, my long-suffering personal assistant who has had to juggle complicated schedules to facilitate the many hours I have had to spend to prepare for the lectures.

Many friends offered ideas and stimulated my thinking. I offer my thanks to Wang Gungwu, Tommy Koh, Leonard Andaya, Barbara Andaya, Gyanesh Kudaisya, Medha Kudaisya, Geraldine Heng, Chan Heng Chee, Edgar Liao, Kwa Chong Guan, Peter Borschberg, Derek Heng, Imran Tajudeen, Albert Lau, Huang Jianli, Kwok Kian Woon and Chua Beng Huat for the things they have taught me through our many conversations and discussions on the history of Singapore.

Finally, I wish to express my gratitude to my family – Sylvia, Benjamin, Cheryl and Ryan – for their love and support. To them, I dedicate this book.

Tan Tai Yong
5 July 2019

ABOUT THE MODERATORS

CHUA Beng Huat is Professor of Social Sciences (Urban Studies) at Yale-NUS College and Professor, Department of Sociology, National University of Singapore (NUS). He was previously Provost Chair Professor, Faculty of Arts and Social Sciences (2009–2017) and Head of the Department of Sociology (2009–2015) at NUS.

Janadas DEVAN is Director of the Institute of Policy Studies. He is concurrently the government's Chief of Communications at the Ministry of Communications and Information, and Deputy Secretary at the Prime Minister's Office.

KWA Chong Guan is Senior Fellow at the S. Rajaratnam School of International Studies at Nanyang Technological University and has an honorary affiliation with the Department of History, NUS.

KWOK Kian-Woon is Associate Provost (Student Life) at Nanyang Technological University (NTU). He has served in the leadership of the NTU School of Humanities and Social Sciences since its inception. His teaching and research interests relate to the historical and comparative understanding of modern social transformation and contemporary social change.

Lydia LIM is Head, Training and Talent Development and Associate Opinion Editor at *The Straits Times*. Since joining the paper in 1999, she has covered local politics, policies and Singapore-Malaysia relations.

YATIMAN Yusof is High Commissioner (Non-Resident) of Singapore to Kenya and Member of the Singapore Bicentennial Advisory Panel. He is also Adjunct Professor and Programme Advisor of the School of Humanities and Behavioural Sciences at Singapore University of Social Sciences.

Lecture I

THE LONG AND SHORT OF SINGAPORE HISTORY
Cycles, Pivots and Continuities

Introduction

In 2019 Singapore will mark the bicentennial of the arrival of the British — in the person of Thomas Stamford Raffles. Major historical anniversaries provide an impetus for historians, as well as the general public, to reassess the way certain events or individuals have been written about and remembered, or excluded and forgotten. They also offer a chance for official political and historical narratives to be reinforced or reframed. Thus, when it was announced that the bicentennial would be commemorated, it was not surprising that questions were asked if we should be celebrating a "founding" by a British imperialist, and whether we should be proud of the fact that, from 1819 to 1963, Singapore was ruled as a colony. There were other concerns: should we still be wedded to the idea that all our history began in 1819, and that we have no meaningful past before the arrival of Raffles? Not unexpectedly, the organisers of the Singapore Bicentennial commemoration have been at pains to stress that, "rather than a celebration, the bicentennial is a time to reflect on the nation's journey." There are plans for projects that will explore the 500 years before 1819 to allow the "full complexities of history" to emerge.[1]

---

[1] "Singapore's Bicentennial Commemoration in 2019: A Time to Reflect on its Rich History," *Channel NewsAsia*, 31 December 2017, https://www.channelnewsasia.com/news/singapore/singapore-s-bicentennial-commemoration-in-2019-a-time-to-reflect-9823248.

Historicising is, of course, never straightforward. Interpretations of Singapore's past have been freighted with questions and contention over openness, access to official records, and omissions. Several opinion pieces in the Chinese and English broadsheets have asked how we should be engaging our history. One opined, "all societies cannot avoid an inherent tension between history and politics, but the mature and correct attitude lies in respecting historical facts while retaining an openness towards all possible interpretations of those facts." It adds, "only by having an open-minded attitude towards history, can we better understand and employ it as a compass for the future." Another argued that the "freedom to grapple with and understand history on one's own terms would be a mark of society's maturity and liberalisation." Writing for *The Straits Times*, Elgin Toh hoped that the bicentennial would provide an opportunity to fully explore Singapore's past, both the good and the bad.[2]

So, my tenure as the S R Nathan Fellow for the coming year is timed, I believe, to contribute to an ongoing conversation about our history. I shall use the opportunity to share my thoughts as a historian and to suggest ways to understand our history. Ultimately, I hope to stimulate thinking about our past and how knowledge of history could help us reflect on our identities as an individual, society and country.

A small caveat before I begin. I am not a historian of Singapore. I started my academic life specialising in South Asian history, and did my doctoral work at Cambridge University on colonial Punjab. My earlier publications were on the Sikhs, Punjab, and the partition of India. I came to Singapore history a little late, and have had the benefit of learning from several friends and colleagues who have dedicated their careers to studying Singapore history. This series of lectures does not all represent my own original research. They will be a synthesis of a large body of work that has been developed over the past few decades. I will draw on these works, and

---

[2] Editorial opinions in *Lianhe Zaobao* and *The Straits Times*, cited by Huang Jianli, "Bicentennial Commemoration of Raffles' Landing in Singapore: Preparatory Steps and History Dilemmas" (translated), *Yihe Shiji* (Ee Hoe Hean Club publication), no. 36 (July 2018): 8–19.

I wish to thank in advance all the scholars who have helped educate me on Singapore history.

In today's lecture, I will analyse the state of history in the three phases that our history has been written: a post-1965 national narrative, the colonial period, and the longer pre-1819 past. I will then attempt to cast a broader frame to make the case for a connected history marked by cyclical changes, occasional ruptures, significant pivots, and underlying continuities. Singapore has taken many forms, and I will highlight certain consistent dynamics that have shaped its evolution.

The evolving place of history in Singapore

Now, let me start at the beginning — well, at one of the beginnings — and not of the history of Singapore, but of the national project of writing the history of Singapore as a nation state. This conceptual differentiation between history as a set of events and the writing of history is key to understanding why the official history of Singapore is the way it is, why it will inevitably and always be contested, and how it has evolved and will have to continue to evolve.

The writing of an official history and a people's experience of this history are not unique to Singapore. The writing of history is done by subjective human beings. These are fallible individuals relying on imperfect and incomplete information, with their particular personal biases and perspectives, who reflect the needs and values, as well as hopes and fears of their society. This influences their identification of salient facts and colours their presentation. The British historian E.H. Carr concluded, "History is an unending dialogue between the present and the past." The historian, he said, "starts with a provisional selection of facts, and a provisional interpretation in the light of which that selection has been made — by others as well as by himself."[3] Appreciating this, we can better understand how the official story of Singapore as a nation state has solidified into a

---

[3]   E.H. Carr, *What is History?* (Penguin Books, [1961] 2018).

dominant narrative that goes like this: Singapore was an "accidental nation"; its birth was beset with existential challenges, and the ensuing story is one of struggle for survival and success.

No use for history

In fact, in the first few years of independence, we did not have much of an official history. History, or history writing, was not an urgent priority for the People's Action Party (PAP) government. The immediate needs were to establish the state and government, stabilise the economy, ensure social harmony, and survive challenges to its independence in a tough neighbourhood. There was no time to mull over the past, or worry about recording the present for the future.[4] History could not contribute to the priority of nation building and economic growth. In fact, the past, especially the recent past, was regarded as an obstacle to Singapore's progress, and so Singaporeans were exhorted to look to the future instead. For Singapore's political leadership, dwelling on Singapore's past could lead our people back to primeval ties of race, and older allegiances to tribe and faith. These were seen as sources of Singapore's social and political vulnerability, rather than strengths. For then Secretary-General of the National Trades Union Congress Devan Nair, the dark past was to be differentiated from the ordered and hopeful present, with the turning point being PAP rule.[5]

Reconsidering history with the benefit of hindsight

However, from the early 1980s, the government grew concerned about Singaporeans' understanding of national history. Singapore had survived its tumultuous early years and done well economically, but this also meant

---

[4] Albert Lau, "Nation-Building and the Singapore Story: Some Issues in the Study of Contemporary Singapore History," in *Nation-Building: Five Southeast Asian Histories*, ed. Wang Gungwu (Singapore: Institute of Southeast Asian Studies, 2005), 224.

[5] Hong Lysa and Huang Jianli, *The Scripting of a National History: Singapore and its Pasts* (Singapore: NUS Press, 2008), 52.

that the Singapore of the 1980s was quite different from the Singapore that had exited the Malaysian Federation. Singapore leaders were now worried that Singapore's rapid transformation and development would mean that its young had no grasp of the past. Singapore's young lacked personal recollections of the turbulent colonial and Malaysian era (1963–65) of Singapore, and had gone through less hardship than their parents and grandparents. The leaders feared that Singaporeans would start to take Singapore's existence and success for granted.

The first official historical narrative focused on a generally benign and progressive colonial administration, the political changes that led to the establishment of the PAP government, a short period of post-independence economic struggle, regaining of socio-economic stability, and an optimistic growth trajectory. In reality, the making of this simple tale was anything but simple. For instance, the place of Raffles in Singapore's history was briefly in doubt in Singapore's early post-independence years. There had not been consensus among the first generation of PAP leaders over whether or not to retain Raffles as a key part of Singapore's historical narrative. While then Second Deputy Prime Minister S Rajaratnam declared in 1984 that "nominating Raffles as the founder of modern Singapore [was] accepting a fact of history", he acknowledged that there had been debate over this given the PAP's anti-colonial roots.[6] Singapore's attitude towards our colonial past was not one of straightforward acceptance, and it has continued to evolve. Beyond this simple history, Singapore's past had its fair share of difficult, contentious moments — there were the vicissitudes of colonialism, political transitions, racial tensions, fierce ideological contestation, and merger with and separation from Malaysia. But while the attenuated official narrative would appear inadequate today, it is understandable when we consider the contemporary context.

---

[6] S Rajaratnam, "Speech by Mr S Rajaratnam, Second Deputy Prime Minister (Foreign Affairs), at a seminar on 'Adaptive Reuse: Integrating Traditional Areas into the Modern Urban Fabric' held at the Shangri-La Hotel, April 28, 1984 at 10.30am," National Archives of Singapore, http://www.nas.gov.sg/archivesonline/speeches/record-details/79c7d80b-115d-11e3-83d5-0050568939ad.

History with purpose: Nation-building

The shift in the authorities' attitude in the 1980s meant that history, formerly dropped from the primary school curriculum in favour of more "useful studies" directed at Singapore's industrial needs,[7] was now reinstated. Numerous political leaders reiterated the importance of remembering Singapore's uncertain beginnings and the lessons of other nations' rise and decline, in order to sustain Singapore's existence and prosperity.[8]

National Education (NE) was introduced into Singapore's curriculum from 1997. It was to be implemented across subjects in the formal curriculum, with history being just one of them.[9] The Ministry of Education's justification for NE was that school-going Singaporeans were largely unaware of Singapore's past, association with Malaysia, and demonstrated little interest in nation building.[10] Thus, NE set out to make sure that students were acquainted with basic knowledge of key moments in Singapore's national history, and to strengthen students' sense of national identity and emotional attachment to Singapore.[11] According to then Deputy Prime Minister Lee Hsien Loong, the Singapore Story that was to be taught under NE was "objective history, seen from a Singaporean standpoint."[12] The introduction of NE curriculum was timed closely with the staging of the exhibition *The Singapore Story: Overcoming the Odds,* and the launch of then Senior Minister Lee Kuan Yew's first volume of memoirs, *The Singapore Story: Memoirs of Lee Kuan Yew.* According to the senior Lee, he had written his memoirs because he was "troubled by the over-confidence of a generation that has only known stability, growth

---

[7] Lau, "Nation-Building and the Singapore Story," 224.

[8] Ibid., 227.

[9] Lee Hsien Loong, "Speech by BG (NS) Lee Hsien Loong, Deputy Prime Minister, at the Launch of National Education at Television Corporation of Singapore (TCS) TV Theatre on Friday, 17 May 1997 at 9.30am," National Archives of Singapore, http://www.nas.gov.sg/archivesonline/speeches/record-details/77e6b874-115d-11e3-83d5-0050568939ad.

[10] Lau, "Nation-Building and the Singapore Story," 228.

[11] Lee Hsien Loong, "Speech at the Launch of National Education."

[12] Ibid.

and prosperity."[13] His memoirs, while personal, were presented as an authoritative history. Together, these developments reinforced history's place on Singapore's nation-building agenda.

History with purpose: Legitimising a system of governance

The Singapore Story has since become inextricably tied to Lee's account of his experience of that history as the key player, with the PAP as Singapore's dominant political force post-independence. For the PAP, Singapore's success has vindicated its pragmatic rather than populist decision-making and its continued role as Singapore's dominant political force. The PAP had worked with its opponents reluctantly, if only to ensure Singapore's transition from colonialism to self-government.[14] This account of Singapore's early nation-building years served to buttress the legitimacy of the government of the day and its system of governance.

Indeed, in one of the earliest articulations of this story, by S Rajaratnam, Singapore's first foreign minister, the PAP was an innocent novice pitted against more experienced but ill-intentioned groupings. Rajaratnam's "PAP's First Ten Years", which appeared in the *PAP Tenth Anniversary Celebration Souvenir 1964*, provided the first signed account of internal party history by a PAP leader and minister.[15] It legitimised the PAP in opposition to its political foes. This narrative has since become a template not just for the PAP, but for Singapore history, too.[16]

Like other national histories, Singapore's was written to inform readers of their nation's past, and to highlight its relevance for the present. The Singapore Story of the PAP's leadership emerging as public figures became a reference point for understanding the present.[17] Past and present

---

[13] Lee Kuan Yew, *The Singapore Story: Memoirs of Lee Kuan Yew* (Singapore: Times Edition, 1998), 8.

[14] Hong and Huang, *The Scripting of a National History*, 3.

[15] Reproduced in Kwa Chong Guan and S Rajaratnam, "PAP's First Ten Years," in *S Rajaratnam on Singapore: From Ideas to Reality* (Singapore: World Scientific, 2006), 180–226.

[16] Hong and Huang, *The Scripting of a National History*, 48–49.

[17] Ibid., 6.

PAP leaders have been portrayed as firm, capable and having foresight. Supporting this portrayal is the basic dominant narrative built around the role of the PAP and Lee Kuan Yew, and a teleology of progress from adversity to success. As a former graduate student of the history department wrote, "a Martian with only the official script would think there is only one political movement — the PAP; two important personalities in Singapore — Stamford Raffles and Lee Kuan Yew; and three dates — 1819, 1942 and 1965 — that are worth remembering."[18]

Singapore's straight-arrow trajectory, beginning with Raffles

So Singaporeans grew up believing that Singapore's story started in 1819, with the landing of Raffles, and that colonialism brought many benefits — modern infrastructure, people, and wealth through trade. The modern state of Singapore was apparently built on the benefits of colonialism while overcoming many of its downsides. This is best illustrated by the decision to retain, rather than cast Raffles' statue into the Singapore River. Lee Kuan Yew revealed in his memoirs that it was Albert Winsemius, Singapore's then economic advisor, who suggested that letting the statue of Raffles remain would indicate a public acceptance of Britain's colonial legacy and send a positive signal to investors. Even as Rajaratnam acknowledged in the 1980s the irony of the PAP selecting Raffles as the nation's founder given its anti-colonial roots, the party had deemed it the best choice.[19]

Thus, unlike most postcolonial states, Singapore enthusiastically embraced its colonial past. Pragmatism drove this decision, which served as a starting point in the Singapore Story. Further, there was a concern that, given Singapore's multi-racial population, people would tend to go back to their primeval roots, leading possibly to racial tensions and polarisation. The political leaders thus decided that the most neutral party that could

---

[18] Liew Kai Khiun, 2006, cited in Hong and Huang, *The Scripting of A National History*, 15.

[19] Hong and Huang, *The Scripting of a National History*, 16. S Rajaratnam gave two speeches: one about the choice of Raffles as Singapore's founder at the 160th anniversary of Raffles Institution in 1983; another on the occasion of a national exhibition commemorating 25 years of self-government in 1984.

unite Singaporeans and support the building of national identity would be the British. It helped that Singapore had not gone through a bloody period of mass nationalist movement or revolution, unlike many of its regional counterparts.

The decision was made to present Singapore's story as a straight-arrow trajectory, with clear positive outcomes. And this is how we arrived at the familiar refrains — "from colony to nation", the "struggle for success", and "from Third World to First". In many senses, this trajectory is not inaccurate. The story from 1965 was indeed one of significant growth and development. Use any economic and social indicator to compare Singapore between 1965 and 2015, and the story of amazing growth is immediately obvious. There were also the values that went into that success story — resilience, meritocracy, good governance, multiculturalism. These values and attitudes could then bind Singapore's different ethnic groups together on the level of ideology.[20] "Asian values" were interwoven into Singapore's national narrative and included in the National Education curriculum in schools.

Beyond the best fit line: Edges and nuances

From a state and nation-building perspective in Singapore's early years, the adoption of this straight-arrow trajectory made sense. But Lee Kuan Yew admitted in 1983 that "the past 24 years were not pre-ordained. Nor is the future .... There will be unexpected problems ahead, as there were in the past."[21]

The way Singapore society and government are arranged and constituted, and their values, have their basis in historical and contemporary challenges. However, this is not always clear, particularly during a period of prolonged peace and stability. Thus, a deeper analysis and interrogation of

---

[20] Ien Ang and Jon Stratton, "The Singapore Way of Multiculturalism: Western Concepts/Asian Cultures", *Sojourn* 10, no. 1 (April 1995): 76.

[21] Lee Kuan Yew, "Speech by Prime Minister Lee Kuan Yew at His 60th Birthday," September 16, 1983, http://www.nas. gov.sg/archivesonline/speeches/record-details/73f6398a-115d-11e3-83d5-0050568939ad.

the sources of Singapore's strengths and weaknesses is due. If the current narrative survives this review, then it would be on a firmer foundation. If it is shown to be inadequate, it needs to be renewed, changed and buttressed.

Indeed, as time passes, Singaporeans are asking more questions, and want to know more. Was the main narrative glossing over elements of our history that we did not have much knowledge of? Has our history been dominated by the stories of the winners? What about others whose histories have fallen by the wayside? Should we not know about those historical actors as well? Why is all history political history — what about social history, cultural history? What about the history of places, of neighbourhoods that are changing because of rapid development?

There are calls, for instance, for more comprehensive and nuanced accounts of the anti-colonial and left-wing movement of the 1950s. While the political battles between the PAP and its left-wing rivals have been reprised as part of the Singapore Story and in the memoirs of participants wishing to give voice to their side of the story, it is perhaps timely for historians, given the passage of time and distance from the dictates of the Cold War, to carefully historicise the events of the 1950s. Analysis should be done in the context of the period and its environment, which saw the interplay of many factors, including international communism, anti-colonialism, security calculations, merger with Malaya, power struggles, ideological contestations, and differing visions for the future of Singapore.

To focus on single-cause explanations for actions and events, or to cast judgement purely on the basis of hindsight, is to miss the opportunity for a deeper understanding of and reflection on an important and defining episode of our recent past. Instead, what we need is solid historical research. This in turn will be made possible by the opening of official archives and sources, which will provide good materials for studies.

A dominant national narrative might be necessary for national education, but a good way of building historical consciousness is to instil it at a personal level, and grow it organically. This can be done in schools but also through self-discovery. Each of us needs to know our country through grandfather or grandmother stories. At the same time, there should always be space for personal recollections and individual reflections that are not strictly historical studies. These can be essential elements for a larger, multifaceted story that is the history of Singapore.

We are now seeing a renewed interest in studying Singapore's history more closely, from different perspectives, and at different levels. Our current official history is arguably not sufficiently fit for purpose and perhaps even its purpose of nation building needs to be re-examined and expanded. I hope that this effervescence can find space and support in various forms. Certainly, it is not sufficient to start understanding Singapore's history from 1965. So I turn to another beginning — our colonial history.

Singapore's colonial history

As I mentioned earlier, unlike most former colonies, Singapore embraced its colonial past in largely positive terms — the period of British rule having been co-opted into the Singapore Story. However, Singapore's colonial past did not always fit neatly into a narrative.

As this narrative goes, modern Singapore dates from 1819, when the British arrived on the island, signed a preliminary treaty with the Temenggong of Johor, and proceeded to set up a trading post. Colonial exceptionalism — to wit, Singapore's transformation in the 19th century into a successful port city, the Japanese Occupation, the political struggles of the 1950s and 1960s, have their place within a teleological framework. It explains events and actions as either impeding or aiding the attainment of nationhood, and thereafter Singapore's progress from Third World to First under the PAP government.

However, early postcolonial sensibilities and the historical baggage attached to colonialism make this period in Singapore's history less amenable to being incorporated smoothly into the nationhood narrative. Here is Rajaratnam in 1987, speaking at the opening of an exhibition organised by the National Museum Art Gallery:

Most of the 170 years [sic] history following Raffles' purchase of this island for a few thousand Mexican dollars is not something Singaporeans like to proclaim from the housetops, because all of that history was British colonial history. The only proven history Singapore had was in the eyes of most nationalists a shameful episode of exploitation, oppression and humiliation of a people who nevertheless insisted on remaining in Singapore. Patriotism required that we performed some sort of collective lobotomy to wipe out all traces of 146 years of shame ....

After Singapore became independent there was agitation that the statue of a brooding Raffles in front of Victoria Memorial Hall should be torn down and flung into the Singapore River to symbolically reject our past.

Fortunately, sanity prevailed in the nick of time. Not only was Raffles' death by drowning commuted but, by way of apology, he now has a twin brother brooding beside a Singapore River now free of industrial and other waste. Unfortunately, the passion to wipe out 146 years of shameful history until quite recently burnt unabated in the iconoclastic hearts of our single-minded city planners, unreal estate developers, businessmen, bankers and others who had decided that Singapore's history should start from 1965 and that everything in our city should not be older than 20 years ....

There is a Singapore history — the only history which we have and which can explain why we are what we are and why we must be different from our alien and distant cousins whose less adventurous fathers, wisely or unwisely elected to miss the immigrant's boat.[22]

---

[22] S Rajaratnam, "Speech by S Rajaratnam, Senior Minister (Prime Minister's Office) at the official opening of the exhibition 'A Vision of the Past' at the National Museum Art Gallery on Thursday, 14 May 1987 at 6.10pm," http://www.nas.gov.sg/archivesonline/speeches/record-details/723c23ee-115d-11e3-83d5-0050568939ad.

Today, Rajaratnam's quote would undoubtedly throw up critiques, especially from a postcolonial perspective. It demonstrates how Singapore's colonial past has been appropriated to set the stage for the post-1965 story and cement the PAP's place in history. I am interested in locating these views within a broader discussion on how Singapore's past has been constructed and presented.

In their book, *The Scripting of a National History: Singapore and Its Pasts*, historians Hong Lysa and Huang Jianli discuss the motivation behind the writing of an official history for the purpose of nation building. They argue that, in the aftermath of Singapore's acrimonious separation from Malaysia in August 1965:

> *An autonomous history of Singapore was eschewed as emphasising the different and divided ancestries and loyalties of the migrant population, which thus was best forgotten. Rejecting the option of scripting a credible pre-colonial past for fear that the price would be nativist claims on the part of the Malays [who] formed around 18 per cent of the population, which would alienate those with forebears from China (75 per cent) and India (6 per cent), the government decided to look towards an unencumbered future instead.*[23]

The writing of the history of *modern* Singapore thus traced its roots to 1819 and drew on the legacy of colonial exceptionalism.

With Singapore history returning to the school curriculum, a narrative had to be found. The inaugural edition of the two-volume history textbook drew on the structure and themes suggested by historian Mary Turnbull. Published in 1977, her book, *A History of Singapore: 1819–1975*, was not the first attempt at writing a history of Singapore. But it was "the first [to be] conceived as a history textbook for the newly emerging Singapore nation

---

[23] Hong and Huang, *The Scripting of a National History*, 4–5.

state."[24] Gone was the focus on world history and ancient civilisations stretching from 500 BC.[25] No longer would the history of Singapore be "taught simply as a brief appendage of the history of Malaya."[26] Singapore's history now started with the arrival of Raffles in 1819 and led to independence in 1965. Turnbull's narrative can be seen as the precursor to the Singapore Story, which emerged in the 1990s, and has since established itself as the dominant version of the nation's history.

Postcolonial writing of Singapore's colonial history

Historiographical shifts in the writing of Singapore's colonial history did not take place in isolation from broader external developments. An older generation of history students trained at the University of Malaya viewed Singapore as a part of the larger British empire. Their history of Malaya and Singapore was gleaned from the archived records of the East India Company and the Colonial Office. After World War II, the writing of history underwent changes as Marxist and social history took root, as did the Annales school of thought. In the field of Southeast Asian studies, the idea of an autonomous history of Southeast Asia, a history written from within, was advocated by John Smail and Harry Benda in the 1960s. Cultural history followed in the 1970s and the 1980s.

As subsequent generations of Singapore students and scholars took up the study of history here and overseas, they were exposed to these historiographical trends, which in turn shaped the way they approached Singapore's colonial history. Calling for the moving of historical gaze away from the high politics of the colonial state, historian Dipesh Chakrabarty said:

---

[24] Kevin Blackburn, "Mary Turnbull's History Textbook for the Singapore Nation," in *Studying Singapore's Past: C.M. Turnbull and the History of Modern Singapore*, ed. Nicholas Tarling, (Singapore: NUS Press, 2012), 66.

[25] Ibid., 69–70. See also, Hong and Huang, *The Scripting of a National History*, 5–6.

[26] Blackburn, "Mary Turnbull's History Textbook," 69.

> *Consider for a moment what the results have been of incorporating into the discourse of history the pasts of groups such as the working classes and women. History has not been the same ever since a Thompson or a Hobsbawm took up his pen to make the working class look like major actors in society, or since the time feminist historians made us realise the importance of gender relations and of the contributions of women to critical social processes.*[27]

Similarly, the telling of Singapore's history has evolved. From just featuring "'pioneer' Asians, immigrants-made-good and businessmen who became community leaders",[28] there was a trend in the late 1980s towards the writing of "history from below". This endeavoured to give voice and agency to the voiceless and marginalised, and to ordinary people. Two notable works in this vein were written by the American historian James Francis Warren — *Rickshaw Coolie: A People's History of Singapore, 1880–1940*, which was published in 1986, and *Ah Ku and Karayuki-san: Prostitution in Singapore 1870–1940* in 1993.

Over the years, historians have adapted their methods by turning to other disciplines, such as anthropology. Oral history, literature and literary thought are increasingly used, in addition to archival sources such as census reports and maps. Many historians have also heeded calls for the use of non-English vernacular sources, to widen their scope of research. Historians exploring Singapore's past are using new lines of enquiry and finding new ways of framing it.

The focus on the study of the colonial past thus far has been on local developments, but historians have also been looking at broader developments such as the emergence of networks driven by empire.

---

[27] Dipesh Chakrabarty, "Minority Histories, Subaltern Pasts," in *Economic and Political Weekly* 33 no. 9 (February 28, 1998), 473.

[28] Karl Hack, "Framing Singapore's History," in *Studying Singapore's Past: C. M. Turnbull and the History of Modern Singapore*, ed. Nicholas Tarling (Singapore: NUS Press, 2012), 33.

A productive and useful approach to the study of colonial pasts has been proposed by historian Tony Ballantyne. He explains in his work, *Orientalism and Race*:

> *The British empire, as much as a spider's web, was dependent on these inter-colonial exchanges. Important flows of capital, personnel and ideas between colonies energized colonial development and the function of the larger imperial system.*[29]

The metaphor of the web, he argues, holds several advantages for our study of the imperial past. "It underscores the idea that the empire was a structure, a complex fabrication fashioned out of a great number of disparate parts (colonies) that were brought together into a new relationship."[30] Adopting such a framework allows historians to uncover networks and flows of personnel, capital and ideas between colonies, which had previously been obscured when colonialism was examined mainly as a metropole-focused history or histories of individual colonies.

The study of Singapore would benefit from an approach where developments are examined within the context of inter-colonial exchanges, as well as network flows across long periods of time and distances.

Recalibrating the starting point of Singapore's history

The emphasis on networks and connections also brings to mind ebbs and flows in history, such as the case of Singapore's pre-colonial past. Rajaratnam has said of the period, "What happened before 1819 — if anything worthwhile happened at all — has been irretrievably lost in the mists of time."[31] He was not alone in his views. K. G. Tregonning, who

---

[29] Tony Ballantyne, *Orientalism and Race: Aryanism in the British Empire* (Basingstoke: Palgrave Macmillan, 2006), 15.

[30] Tony Ballantyne, *Webs of Empire: Locating New Zealand's Colonial Past* (Vancouver, UBC Press, 2014), 45–46.

[31] S Rajaratnam, cited in Kwa Chong Guan, *Pre-Colonial Singapore* (Singapore: Institute of Policy Studies, National University of Singapore and Straits Times Press, 2017), 7.

was Raffles Professor of History, declared in an essay, "Modern Singapore began in 1819. Nothing that occurred on the island prior to this has particular relevance to an understanding of the contemporary scene; it is of antiquarian interest only."[32]

The history of modern Singapore may have started in the 19th century, but to insist that everything that happened before is irrelevant is inaccurate. A Braudelian, *longue durée* approach to the study of Singapore history will help uncover long-term change and continuity, which does not foreground 1819 or 1965 as definitive episodes. Rather, the 200 years of colonial rule can be seen as a period in a longer cycle of developments that can be traced all the way back to the 14th century.

The pre-1819 narrative

Since the 1990s, through the efforts of historians like John Miksic, Kwa Chong Guan, Peter Borschberg, Derek Heng, and Imran Tajudeen, to name a few, our historical perspective has broadened, with the chronology extending to include Singapore's pre-1819 past. We have been able to develop a clearer picture of a long stretch of Singapore's history, long before the arrival of Raffles. With evidence from a combination of archaeological material, classical texts like the *Sejarah Melayu*, regional court chronicles, the writings of early travellers to Southeast Asia, Chinese and European accounts, and cartography, we can no longer accept what Rajaratnam had argued before, that Singapore "has no long past." Historians are now able to show that Singapore has a longer history — however disjointed — that stretched back to the 14th century, during which there were activities that Singapore either had a presence in itself, or had a part to play, such as the maritime activities around the region. Such an account of Singapore's longer past needs to transcend the nation state paradigm, and has to be understood in the context of local conditions, regional changes and transformations.

---

[32] Ibid., 7.

Let me briefly sketch out the story of pre-1819 Singapore, as we know it now.[33]

14th-century Temasek

Archaeological evidence shows that there were land settlements and differentiated space usage on the island from around the late 13th century. Information gleaned from Chinese historical texts, Malay oral traditions, colonial accounts and archaeological data allow historians to reconstruct an urban settlement around Fort Canning Hill that included a palace precinct, the existence of a wall encompassing the port city, and a settlement on the north bank of the Singapore River. Singapore's history may be said to have begun in that period. This is not to suggest there was no settlement before the 14th century, but merely that there is no evidence pertaining to any settlement of historical consequence before that date.

The polity that existed in the 14th century, which was then called Temasek, faded out towards the end of that century, caused by a multitude of factors that included environmental exigencies and shifts in the power configuration of the region. But Singapore did not disappear altogether. As the island's settlement lost its political autonomy, owing to the rise of new regional powers in Siam and Java, and an ascendant Ming China, it became part of the Melaka Sultanate. The island's inhabitants, in particular the various Orang Laut groups, became integrated as part of the larger Melayu body-politic, with its leaders having a place in the Melakan court. The port in Singapore gradually declined to become a secondary feeder port to the primary emporium of Melaka.

The Melaka sultanate

By the 15th century, Melaka had emerged as "the premier emporium" for

---

[33] The narrative in the ensuing paragraphs is recounted in considerable detail in Kwa Chong Guan, Derek Heng, Peter Borschberg, Tan Tai Yong, *Seven Hundred Years: A History of Singapore* (Singapore: Marshall Cavendish Edition and National Library Board, 2019). See also, John Miksic and Cheryl-Ann Low Mei Gek, *Early Singapore, 1300s–1819: Evidence in Maps, Text and Artefacts* (Singapore: Singapore History Museum, 2004).

the South China Sea and Bay of Bengal trade, a part of the Ming tributary network. According to Anthony Reid, Southeast Asia entered into an "Age of Commerce" from 1450 to 1680.[34] Melaka was a point at which three different commercial networks — from the South China Sea, South Asia and West Asia — converged to trade. It thrived with attractive facilities, port charges and taxes, despite lacking the naval force to control or coerce traders. The Ming Dynasty participated actively in the South China Sea maritime world to satisfy Chinese demand for exotic goods at that time. And to win Chinese favours and secure its position as the primary emporium in the Straits of Melaka, the rulers of Melaka sent tributary missions to the Ming Court in 1405 and 1407, even travelling to the capital Nanjing in 1411.

The Shahbandar's office

Singapore's story took another turn at the beginning of the 16th century, following the Portuguese attack and capture of Melaka in 1511, and the subsequent establishment of the Johor Sultanate as the successor of the Melaka Sultanate. What was Singapore like during this period? Portuguese maps and correspondence in the 16th century referred to a Shahbandar's office located in Singapore, serving as a local intermediary between the Sultan of Johor and foreign merchants (Figure 1). Singapore was then described in Portuguese navigators' reports around the early 1500s as a settlement larger than a village but smaller than a city. Ming ceramics found in Singapore, coupled with Chinese records, showed the significance of the Johor Sultanate in trading networks that stretched from Southeast Asia to China's Quanzhou, and suggested that 16th century Singapore was very much part of that trading network. Cast within the context of the shifting competition between the Johor Sultanate and Aceh for trade and political prestige in the Melaka Straits on one hand, and the emerging presence of the Portuguese and Spanish trading empires, and the Dutch East Indies

---

[34] Anthony Reid, *Southeast Asia in the Age of Commerce, 1450-1680* (New Haven: Yale University Press, 1990).

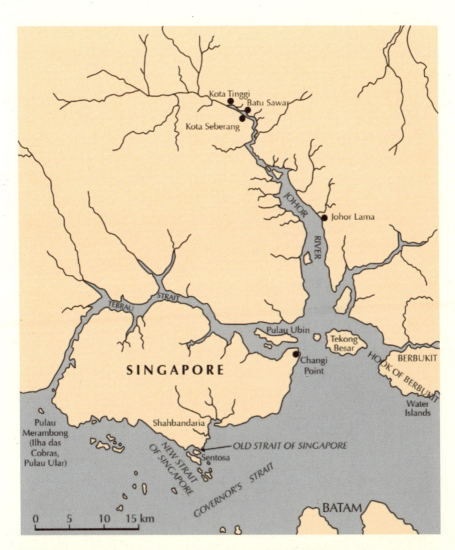

FIGURE 1: Map of the southern part of the Malay peninsula, which shows the various straits around Singapore and historic upstream towns of the Johor River region. Also shown is "Shahbandaria", meaning port master's compound. Portuguese maps and correspondence in the 16th century referred to a Shahbandar's office located in Singapore. *Source:* Kwa Chong Guan, Derek Heng, Peter Borschberg, & Tan Tai Yong, *Seven Hundred Years: A History of Singapore* (Singapore: National Library Board and Marshall Cavendish, 2019), 105.

Company in Southeast Asia and across the South China Sea on the other, Singapore began to take on a dual nature.

As a settlement, it served as a collection centre for the Johor Sultanate and home to a local naval fleet. At the same time, as the trade between East and West became increasingly integrated through the Portuguese, Spanish and Dutch shipping and commercial networks, the waters around Singapore became increasingly important, with the frontiers of western cartographic and navigational knowledge being systematically pushed forward.

Competition around the waters of Singapore

The developments of the 16th century culminated, at the start of the 17th century, in intense conflict and competition in the waters around Singapore. Singapore became the arena of maritime conflict between the naval powers of Europe (Figure 2). Between 1570 and 1630, there was substantial maritime activity around the waters of Singapore, with the Portuguese, Dutch and English trading companies jostling for trading bases that would bolster their strategic presence in the region.

While Singapore's strategic significance to the European powers became increasingly apparent, the habitation history of the island ironically began to fade away. Cursory cartographic and fragmentary archaeological evidence from the early 17th century of the continued existence of a port on the south coast of Singapore (Figure 3) eventually gave way by the mid-17th century, to the absence of any historical documentation of settlement activity on the island. Singapore's history shifted completely from a history driven primarily by activities on land, to one driven primarily by conflict and competition at sea.

By the 18th century, the Dutch had established their base in the Indonesian Archipelago with their headquarters at Batavia. Internal political divisions in the Johor Sultanate court also led to the moving of its capital to the Riau Islands by the late 17th century. The consequent shift of the maritime shipping networks from the southern end of the Melaka Straits further south to the Sunda Straits-Riau-Lingga Archipelago nexus

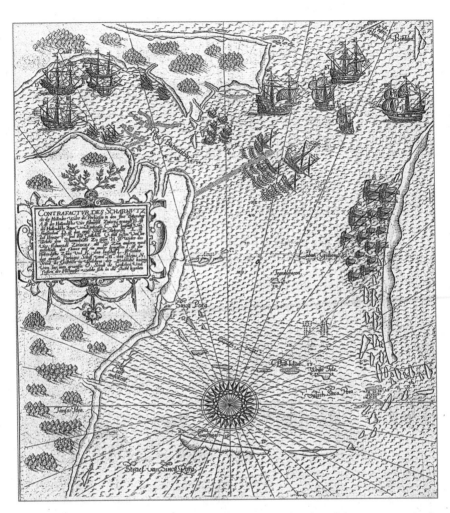

FIGURE 2: Map titled *Chart of a Skirmish between the Dutch and the Portuguese in the Balusabar River* (translated from German). Produced by Theodore de Bry, Johann Theodore de Bry, and Johann Israel de Bry in 1607, it depicts a battle in 1603 between the Dutch and Portuguese on the eastern coast of Singapore. *Source:* National Library, Singapore.

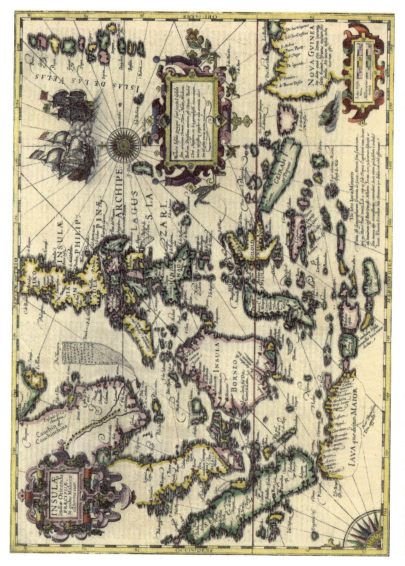

FIGURE 3: Map titled *Insulae Indiae Orientalis* ("The Islands of the East Indies") by Jucodus Hondius, 1606. *Source:* © Peter Borschberg, reproduced from the private collection of Peter Borschberg.

led to the decline of Aceh as a trading centre, and the loss of the strategic importance of the waters around Singapore to international shipping and commerce. This led to the decline in the overall fortunes of the Melaka Straits region and the establishment of the Dutch in the Riau-Lingga Archipelago. It set the regional context for the contestation between the British and the Dutch in the early 19th century, at the cusp of the founding of Singapore by the East India Company.

The Johor sultanate

By this time, the region's centre had shifted to Bintan and Siak, and its trade to the Riaus. The demographics of the Straits of Melaka were changing, with Minangkabau and Bugis diasporas expanding into the peninsula and the Riaus, challenging the old Malay political order. Singapore, as the "site of the social memories about the ancestry of the Malay community", had become increasingly marginalised. The Shahbandar's office in Singapore was shut down, and the sea lanes around the island fell into disuse.

This now led to the part of the history that we are all more familiar with — Temenggong Abdul Rahman and Tengku Hussein welcoming the British presence in Singapore, hoping to establish a new *negeri* in Singapore to rival Bintan. The British were prepared to recognise Tengku Hussein as Sultan of Johor in return for the right to establish a factory on the island, benefitting him in the dynastic politics of the Malay world.

So, in a way, the national narrative was not wrong in suggesting that Singapore was a sparsely populated mangrove swamp when Raffles landed in 1819. But, even Raffles recognised that this had not always been the case on the island that he had chosen to set up a settlement for the East India Company. He knew that the rulers of old Singapore might have been buried in Bukit Larangan — the Forbidden Hill (now Fort Canning) — and chose to build his bungalow there in 1822 so that he could be located in the traditional seat of power as he set up the East India Company settlement.

The long history that I have just outlined presents two main scenarios in Singapore's past — as autonomous societies and settlements on the one hand, and as societies and settlements that were part of a larger entity on the other. Autonomous societies in Singapore have only occurred three times in the past — during the Temasek period (late 13th to 14th centuries), the East India Company Straits Settlement period (1819–1858), and the post-independence period (1965 onwards). This oscillation between being a separate entity and being part of a larger entity is one way of thinking of Singapore's history.

Conclusion

I will round off tonight's lecture with some thoughts on how we can develop a coherent frame of Singapore's history — by viewing an extended period in terms of cycles, pivots and continuities.

Cycles

Historians such as Peter Coclanis[35] have argued that Singapore's history may be framed as a series of cycles that echo repetitively across time, thereby providing continuity and rationality for tying the disjointed periods together.

Inspired by the historical concept of *la longue durée*, this approach is premised on the timelessness of the geographical location of Singapore and set in the natural environment of maritime Asia. Within this contextual framework, Coclanis identified three cycles over the last seven centuries that were anchored upon economic globalisation. These were:

1) The 14th to early 17th centuries, characterised by the rise of the Ming Dynasty and the arrival of European trading nations in maritime Asia;

2) The early 19th to early 20th centuries, characterised by the importance of the China trade to Europe, European imperialism and the establishment of imperial economies on a global scale,

---

[35] Peter Coclanis, *Time's Arrow, Time's Cycle: Globalisation in Southeast Asia Over La Longue Durée* (Singapore: Institute of Southeast Asian Studies, 2006).

and the development of technologies that led to the compression of geographical space; and

3) The 1950s to the present, characterised by the United States-led world economic order and the systematic lowering of barriers to the movement of goods, services and people across national boundaries. This period has seen a further compression of geographical space through the advent of technology.

Applying this to Singapore, Peter Borschberg has identified three different up-cycles — in the 14th century during the period of Temasek, the 16th and 17th centuries under the Johor Sultanate during which time Singapore had a port administered by a Shahbandar's office, and the 19th century through to the present under the British empire and thence under Singapore's independent government.[36]

Kwa Chong Guan, on the other hand, has argued that Singapore's settlement history may be understood as a series of five cyclical echoes centred on the socio-cultural notion of the Melaka Straits regional port-polity, beginning with Srivijaya in Palembang in the late seventh century, followed by Temasek (14th century), Melaka (15th century), Johor (16th–18th centuries), and finally Singapore (19th century to the present).[37]

The above suggest that Singapore may be regarded as part of the cyclical history of a much larger geographical and cultural sphere.

Pivots

Where were the pivots? While the cyclical approach may offer a useful framework for analysis, I should point out that cycles are often spirals, and they do not always return to the same point. At various points in our

---

[36] Peter Borschberg, "Singapore in the Cycles of the Longue Durée," *The Journal of the Malaysian Branch of the Royal Asiatic Society* 90, no.1, June 2017: 30–60.

[37] Kwa Chong Guan, "From Temasek to Singapore: Locating a Global City-State in the Cycles of Melaka Straits History," in *Early Singapore: 1300s–1819*, eds. John Miksic and Cheryl-Ann Low Mei Gek (Singapore: Singapore History Museum, 2004), 124–146.

history, Singapore pivoted away from a particular trajectory, changing its course of history. One could see 1819, for instance, as a pivot away from the Malay world on to something else, and likewise 1965, when we pivoted away again from the region and became a nation state with a global outlook.

Continuities

Yet, underlying this cyclical approach across time and pivots in trajectories is the place of Singapore in a trans-regional setting. Singapore's history bears out the notion that "geography is destiny". In this regard, Singapore's history is continuously linked to its location, which, in turn, determined its role in trans-regional dynamics. In the case of economic globalisation, Singapore finds its place as a commercial nodal point; in the case of the regional socio-cultural mantle of the Malay port-polity, Singapore is the port city with its ruler exercising autonomy, and also influence (*daulat* in Malay) over a large region and the *rakyat* (ordinary people or subjects in Malay) therein.

I am aware that nuances are lost when we take this broad chronological approach to historical narrative. In other words, while economic globalisation could be used to explain the Singapore's history from the late 13th through the early 17th century as a single cycle, the differences between at least three identifiable settlement phases during those three centuries or so cannot be elucidated. It is nonetheless important to assert that Singapore's history needs to be located within the broader regional and international contexts. The critical periods and events in Singapore's past may often be the result of developments that occur much further afield, and over long periods of time.

So, today's lecture sets the stage for my subsequent lectures, which will elaborate on the argument that geography, regional networks, and globalisation are indeed enduring themes in the history of Singapore, and will continue to have a fundamental impact on the present and future of Singapore.

Question-and-Answer Session
Moderated by Mr Yatiman Yusof

Mr Yatiman Yusof: Thank you, Professor Tan Tai Yong, for giving us a very compact 50-minute lecture on the history of Singapore, the thought behind it, the people who were responsible for colouring our history and setting the template, and pointers for our future generations to understand Singapore's history.

You have drawn in your studies from a large body of work developed by earlier scholars specialising in the history of the region. Which areas, in your mind, are insufficiently covered?

Professor Tan Tai Yong: Thank you, Mr Yatiman. I believe there is still a lot of scope for us to develop our history. While there has been a lot of work in the past decades in the writing of Singapore history, there remains a dominant narrative. I think we should be able to pivot somewhat from this dominant narrative, and try to see other aspects of history that are not centred on the Singapore Story. If we want to understand the complexities of Singapore as a society, city-state and nation state, with the kind of history that I just outlined, we have to look at many other things.

I suggested earlier that we might want to relook the period of the 1950s and the early 1960s, because it was an important transitional period, from post-war to when Singapore became entrenched as a nation state, after separation from Malaysia. That was a very critical period where there was a plurality of ideas on where Singapore could be heading. Recognising and understanding the complexities of that time will help us to better understand why a particular path was chosen, or why one political group managed to prevail over others. This will enrich our understanding of how we evolved from a polyglot migrant population after the war to a nation state with a particular trajectory. That is one example. Other areas to examine further include the history of communities, institutions and local neighbourhoods.

I have been very encouraged to see history informing creative works — fiction, literature and art. If we do more of that, we will have a better appreciation that history is not just what we read in textbooks; it is all around us. Each of us has a place in that history and we must own that history. The more we feel that way, the better it is for us as a country going forward.

Mr Yatiman: Now, may I invite questions from the floor, and from outside if there are any? We have quite a sizeable turnout today, and some are watching via video feed in the rooms outside.

Participant: When did the first group of Chinese people settle down in Singapore, and when did the Peranakan culture start?

Prof. Tan: When Wang Dayuan wrote his account of Singapore in the 14th century, he actually made mention of the Chinese already in the midst of the population living north of the Singapore River. He commented that they were living separately from the local population.

So, the evidence would suggest that, from the 14th century, there were already Chinese people settled in Singapore. Then, when Raffles arrived in 1819, there were Chinese gambier planters and others already living on the island. I think in the course of those few hundred years, people were sailing through Singapore and settling here. Ships would come, then wait here for a few months for the monsoons to turn around and sail back. The answer I am giving you is a bit hazy, but the point is that there is evidence of Chinese presence going back all the way to 14th-century Temasek.

The Peranakan culture is tied to this answer. When the Chinese started coming and settling in this part of the world — in Malaya, Singapore, Indonesia — there were intermarriages with the locals that led to the growth of a hybrid culture. I am not able to give you a precise and definitive answer on when it actually started, but Peranakan culture probably evolved over several hundred years.

Mr Yatiman: If you go to Melaka, you can see a place named Bukit Cina. In the 15th century, Sultan Mansur Shah had actually brought in a princess from China known as Hang Li Po, and she settled in Melaka. They had gone through Singapore, one of the Southeast Asian maritime ports. So I think the Chinese were present in Singapore as well as Melaka from early on. On the Peranakan side, I think, unlike Melaka where they have a very distinctive location for the Peranakan community, in Singapore, that was not the case.

Participant: From what you have been saying, Singapore's history must be seen in the context of larger forces, larger countries in the region. At times, if these forces were favourable to us, we prospered, like in the 13th, 14th centuries, and then later when there was a shift, such as when Singapore was attacked by the Thais, the trading patterns shifted away, and we declined. There seemed to be numerous ups and downs. So, projecting that to the future, do you think that we are still very vulnerable to regional powers?

Prof. Tan: The good thing about being a historian is you look backwards only! Indeed, the point of my story is that there will always be ebbs and flows in history. And that any society, Singapore included, cannot be divorced from the forces that function outside its borders.

We are a small port city, and we have evolved from a trading port, to a feeder port, to an emporium, and now, a country. But we are not a country anchored on a civilisation. So the destiny of this place has to be tied to the larger forces that operate outside us. This is something that a lot of people do not appreciate.

I have tried to tell you Singapore's story over 700 years. Project another 700 years into the future and I am quite sure there will be cyclical changes again. Maybe not of the same type or order that we have seen in the past, but there will be the rise and fall of powers again, as well as changing political permutations around the region and elsewhere; these developments will all have an impact on Singapore.

Participant: You mentioned that it might be timely to explore the history of the 1950s and 1960s. But, increasingly, there seems to be slightly more polarised sentiment about this. It almost seems as if anyone who wants to try to better understand the plurality of opinions and options back then is automatically branded anti-establishment and trying to, you know, go against the prevailing narrative. How will we be able to get our people to explore our history in a more academic manner that does not give rise to polarising sentiments?

Prof. Tan: There are some concerns or fears, and, in my view largely unfounded, that the Singapore government does not want us to do research in particular areas. I said that I was a latecomer to Singapore history, but I have written on Singapore history, including a book on the period of Merger between Singapore and Malaya. All these years, I have never been told that I cannot do this or that. I think it is up to me to write what I want to write. When I get on to a project of my choice, I try to be a good historian, which means being intellectually honest, doing proper research, and then defending my position if I have to.

When I wrote the history of Merger, I deliberately did not want to show any of my drafts to the powers that be. I wanted my analysis to be based on my interpretation of the sources I have read. Of course, there was a lot of work to be done; I had to comb through the British colonial archives and the Singapore archives, and try to get as much material as possible to build the narrative and argument. Then I proceeded to write what was, in my view, the most informed account, based on my research and interpretation. When the book was published, I said, well, let it be read and if people challenged my view, I would defend it or, if I am wrong, I will admit I am wrong, and then maybe this will open the space for more research.

Nobody can have the last word on a historical interpretation. And that is how it should be. But, of course, there are challenges. Access to material is one key challenge. This is where, as scholars, we should try to keep pushing for access to the archives. Once that happens, do good, intellectually honest research, and be prepared to be challenged. Also, be humble enough to realise that your interpretation may be wrong, and be prepared to change. I am very sure that there will be many more books on the period of the 1950s and 1960s. As long as you are prepared to do robust, rigorous and comprehensive research, you will be fine. I have supervised many students writing on the 1950s and 1960s, and they were able to do the research they wanted to do, on the topics they were interested in. The only complaint they have sometimes, which I accept, is access to material. But this is a structural thing that you can overcome at some point in time.

Mr Yatiman: If I may add, you should not underestimate the power of the people in shaping history. When I was a student in 1970, I remember that we had a first attempt to educate our schoolchildren on the history of Singapore. The Department of History was asked to write a book entitled, *Our Forefathers: Pioneers of Singapore*. The book came out, but, apparently, some in the community were not very happy with it, and the book was withdrawn. Mind you, this book was supposed to have come from the top, the leadership, but the people did not accept it, they had their own interpretation of history, and they put it on record. I think there has to be that kind of openness when we talk about history.

I have this question coming from the rooms outside. The question is, with 2019 being 200 years since Raffles landed, and Prof. Tan's message that the history of Singapore should and could come from more self-discovery and stories passed down from generations, what message can we share in 2018, ahead of 2019?

Prof. Tan: I believe that one of the approaches that the Singapore Bicentennial Office (SBO) has taken is to try to get histories from the people, so the story they tell would not just be a state-curated one. It will not be a narrative that someone sitting in some ministry is constructing.

The SBO would like to include stories of people, communities, schools and other institutions. Mr Yatiman and I sit on the Bicentennial Advisory Committee, and this is something that we have been advocating from the beginning. It cannot be just a story told by the state. It must also be a story of the people who have been involved in this journey. We hope that there will be many people's stories. So if you are interested to contribute, come and see me after the lecture, and I can give you the contact of the people that you should write to and offer your ideas, and then we will see how they can incorporate them into the overall narrative.

Mr Yatiman: We are encouraging every individual in Singapore to put in writing their personal experience, whether it was going through the Japanese Occupation period, or after Merdeka, and so on.

Prof. Tan: Now, I am going to do a pitch for another project I am heading called, "The Future of Our Pasts". This project was proposed by the Ministry of Education to encourage young people to reflect on Singapore's history. A grant was given to Yale-NUS College, and we are leading this project. There are about 11 projects by young Singaporeans that cover a range of very interesting topics. There is a group of students producing a graphic novel on the declining Kristang language and people finding their identity through that; there is a project on the historical trajectory of public housing in Singapore; and projects covering the love stories of people, schools that have been merged, and changes in neighbourhoods. These projects are spearheaded by young Singaporeans, and what we do is to just give some guidance on historical methods and research. They will be showing their research in early 2019, and this is an example of how history, by the people, can find expression. There are many opportunities for similar research projects.

Participant: What you said just now about opening up the archives, I found very interesting. Would you like to elaborate on that?

Prof. Tan: Well, I could give a full lecture on this. You see, in Singapore, we have a statute that provides for official documents to be transferred to the National Archives after a period of time, and then be declassified and opened up for researchers. Not all ministries observe this provision, for various reasons. Now, I have been involved, along with some of my colleagues sitting in the audience, in trying to declassify official records after a period of 25 to 30 years, and sometimes it is an uphill battle. For reasons of sensitivities, security issues, and other considerations, some agencies explain that they are not able to declassify. So we have to accept that.

But sometimes it is just a simple operational issue, because a lot of organisations and agencies, from my experience, do not know where their archives are! Basically, they have not been systemically archiving their material. I am a faculty member of the History Department at the National University of Singapore and if I were to go to the department now and try to find some files from the 1950s, I may have difficulty locating those materials. We have had a few physical moves, and because we do not have an archiving culture or practice, staff would say, "These are just old files, put them aside or throw them away" and after that they are lost.

Now, with greater consciousness and perhaps a more systematic approach, hopefully we will get it right for the future. It will not be easy, but I think the National Archives and the National Library Board will continue to work with various agencies to see how they can try to declassify as much as possible. I am not trying to present a sanguine kind of situation and say that the records are all there. I believe that it is going to be difficult, because in the last 30 years, things have not been systematically archived.

Participant: I have noticed pre-1819 Singapore history in our school textbooks. Do we think that this is a good move towards a break away from a dominant narrative that we are very used to? Or is there a potential pitfall where we would construct a dominant narrative of pre-1819 Singapore instead?

Prof. Tan: The more we broaden our narrative, chronologically, spatially, the better it is for us, because we then better understand the complexity of our history. I do not think you are going to see the replacement of one dominant narrative with another. As I explained earlier, in the 1960s, 1970s and 1980s, because of the pressures of nation and state building, the government had to construct a story of a straight-arrow trajectory. But as society matures, and as young people like you want to know more, I think the broadening and lengthening of that narrative will become necessary. It may not even stop at 700 years, it may be 800, 900 years when we have more evidence of a longer past. This is what we should be doing all the time, pushing the boundaries of what we know as far as possible. But, at the same time, understanding how all this information fit together is the other challenge. How does it all make sense to us as a country? That is not easy. But I think it would be a happy problem to have, when we have more and more complex stories. Let us deal with it when the time comes, rather than not have a sufficient understanding of our past.

Mr Yatiman: What can people who are not trained in history do to make sense of differing accounts of history?

Prof. Tan: I think what you should do is open your mind and just read as much as you can. And you know, do not just read historical texts by boring historians like me! You should try and engage history in its wider sense. Read popular histories — start with Netflix. Watch the historical dramas, because you learn a lot from those. Then read literature that is based on history. Some of the best historical accounts, in my view, are written by novelists. They are so rich in detail and so beautifully written, they get you hooked. This is the best way to do it: get hooked first. And then you will naturally want to find out more. If you just go for the very dry, academic textbook, it may turn you off, because you say, "There are so many footnotes, I don't know where to start." Get engaged, and then you will find that, actually, history is all around us. Once you enjoy that, the rest should be easy. Start with a good appetiser, so that when the staple comes, you will enjoy it.

Participant: We recently celebrated SG50, and now we have come to the bicentennial. There has been growing interest in history, but to what extent is it influenced by these milestones? How do we sustain this growing interest in history, to build a culture amongst youths especially, to look inwards in Singapore, and in the context of the lecture, consider Singapore and its place in Southeast Asia?

Prof. Tan: I think it is a function of time. In the 1970s, my father never spoke to us about history. He had no time; he was trying to make a living, to pay for his HDB flat. But now, as people become more affluent, as Singaporeans become more mature, more settled, and more confident as a people, they want to know more about their past. I guess governments are always finding anniversaries to celebrate or mark our passage as a country, so SG50 was a very natural one. Now it is the bicentennial.

We should take these as opportunities to pause for a moment and think, "Why 200 years? Why not 700 years? Why are we commemorating it this way and not that way?" As I said at the beginning of my lecture, it is about ways of reflecting and thinking about our history. And on this, I am optimistic. Whether I am leading "The Future of Our Pasts", sitting in the Bicentennial Office, talking to young people, or attending history classes, I always encounter a lot of excitement. This is a good sign that history will flourish. I say, do not be discouraged by unfounded fears that only certain types of histories are allowed in Singapore. Let us try to push the boundaries, and do good history that is based on solid research. I believe there will be a flourishing of historical interpretations. And even if the interpretations vary, that is fine; the world is complex and we must embrace that complexity.

Mr Yatiman: If your statement is a reflection of the mood now, we are very happy that there is an increasing interest in understanding our nation's history. Please join me in thanking Prof. Tan Tai Yong.

Lecture II

CIRCULATIONS, CONNECTIONS AND NETWORKS
Early Globalisation and Cosmopolitan Singapore

Introduction

In my first lecture, I provided an overview of Singapore's 700-year history and suggested ways of framing it. This set the scene for what, in my view, are the enduring themes in Singapore's history over the *longue durée* — geography, regional networks and globalisation. I will argue that these factors have continuously shaped Singapore's fate and fortunes for the past 700 years, and will continue to have an impact on Singapore's present and future.

In this lecture, I shall examine how Singapore experienced the forces of globalisation long before the term came into popular consciousness in the late 20th century. I will also argue that, as a classical port-polity and colonial port city, Singapore had a global orientation and purpose that was nourished by transnational flows and networks.

Rajaratnam's "global city"

Let me begin by making reference to S Rajaratnam again. In 1972, as Minister for Foreign Affairs, he articulated a vision for Singapore as a "global city", an identity that would be realised over three to four decades. He observed, "times are changing and there will be less and less demand for the traditional type of entrepôt services Singapore has rendered for well over a century. Its role as the trading city of South-East Asia, the market place of the region, will become less and less important."[1] In his view, Singapore could no longer hope to sustain its economic growth by serving the needs of Southeast Asia alone. It had to position itself as part of a supply chain of goods and services for a much larger, global market.

Political and geo-strategic realities also prompted Singapore to look beyond Southeast Asia. In an interview with the *Time* bureau chief in 1969, Lee Kuan Yew expressed hopes that Southeast Asia would experience "constructive development", and that Singapore could act as a "spark plug" for the progress and development of the region. He expressed concern that the region could go the other way, towards chaos and destruction, in which case he hoped that Singapore could play the role of Venice when the Dark Ages descended on Europe.[2] In fact, Southeast Asia presented too many problems to become a bastion of stability and growth for Singapore during that period. Relations with Malaysia remained fraught following Separation in 1965, and the race riots of 1969 in Kuala Lumpur was a stark reminder that the underlying tensions that had led to Separation a few years earlier had not wholly subsided. While Konfrontasi had ended, Indonesia was still finding its feet, emerging from the throes of domestic upheavals. The war in Vietnam was entering a critical stage with uncertain outcomes, and Indo-China remained the cockpit of Cold War tensions in Southeast Asia. The formation of ASEAN in 1967 was an attempt to find political stability amidst these geostrategic challenges, but the economic possibilities in the region were not promising. Singapore had to find a way to leapfrog the region for economic growth.

What made the Global City, as envisioned in 1972, so different from the cities that came before it? According to Rajaratnam, a global city, or

---

[1] S Rajaratnam. "Text of Address Titled 'Singapore: Global City', by Mr S Rajaratnam, Minister for Foreign Affairs, to the Singapore Press Club on February 6, 1972." National Archives of Singapore, 6 February 1972.

[2] Hugh D.S. Greenway, "Interview with Prime Minister Mr. Lee Kuan Yew," June 10, 1969, http://www.nas.gov.sg/archivesonline/data/pdfdoc/lky19690610.pdf

"Ecumenopolis", would be a "world-embracing city". Cities of the past, in contrast, had been "isolated centres of local civilisations and regional empires", and "somewhat parochial with an extremely limited range of influence."[3]

Thus, while Singapore's size and links to its region would remain part of its identity, it would connect with other cities in the world, and make "the world ... its hinterland":

> *Global Cities, unlike earlier cities, are linked intimately with one another. Because they are more alike they reach out to one another through the tentacles of technology. Linked together they form a chain of cities which today shape and direct, in varying degrees of importance, a world-wide system of economics. It is my contention that Singapore is becoming a component of that system — not a major component but a growingly important one.*

Painting a picture of a hopeful future, Rajaratnam asserted that the trend towards global cities would benefit Singapore. Many might have assumed that "an independent Singapore would be a self-contained city state", or at most "a regional city ... [whose] fate and fortunes would depend wholly on the economic climate in the region."[4] Instead, Singapore was now on the cusp of realising its potential, which extended beyond the confines of its immediate neighbourhood. Singapore would soon, in Rajaratnam's words, "draw sustenance .... from the international economic system to which as a Global City we belong and which will be the final arbiter of whether we prosper or decline." Expressing confidence in the future of cities, he asserted that, "nothing short of a total collapse of world civilisation can halt the take-over of the world by cities."[5]

---

[3] S Rajaratnam, "Singapore: Global City," in *S Rajaratnam on Singapore: From Ideas to Reality*, ed. Kwa Chong Guan (Singapore: World Scientific, 2006), 230.

[4] Ibid., 232.

[5] Ibid., 231.

What did this shift towards being a global city entail? There would need to be increased connectivity, both physical and technological. According to Rajaratnam, Singapore's port was one crucial link to the world. But it alone could not turn Singapore into a global city, capable of overcoming its lack of natural resources and its small domestic market. Singapore's air traffic would have to grow tremendously if Singapore was to be closely connected to other global cities, like London, Tokyo and New York. Connectivity was also viewed in terms of cable and satellite communications, the international financial network (including Singapore's position as "an important gold market centre"), and collaboration with multinational corporations.

The level of connectivity that Singapore could aspire towards, thanks to technology, marked a departure from its past, where Singapore's strongest overseas links were regional. Rajaratnam was visionary in conceiving of Singapore as being "linked intimately" with a network of global cities, even if they were not geographically close to Singapore.

But Singapore's connections with the rest of the world had long been key to its well-being. Rajaratnam and the Singapore government demonstrated confidence in a vision that had yet to fully materialise. He spoke of transformation — changing Singapore to something it was not. This is perhaps historically inaccurate. Singapore was an internationally connected port city for a long part of its history. The inspiration for the vision of Singapore as a global city, in my view, lay in the past — it rested on 700 years of connections with and comfort in engaging the wider world. This was an engagement that went deep in time. In many ways, this was a return to the past.

Forms and drivers of early globalisation in Southeast Asia

The term globalisation became popular in the 1990s as the preferred explanation for the multiplicity of the supranational forces that had imprinted themselves on the contemporary world. A large and illuminating literature on the economics, politics and sociology of the phenomenon now lies readily at hand. Historians have shown how globalisation has evolved and taken many forms in history, in stages that have been categorised as archaic, proto, modern and postcolonial forms of globalisation. These so-called phases of globalisation, which overlapped and interacted with one another, were driven by similar impulses. Referring to early globalisation, historian Christopher Bayly explained that "globalising networks were created by great kings and warriors searching for wealth and honour in fabulous lands, by religious wanderers and pilgrims seeking traces of God in distant realms, and by merchant princes and venturers pursuing profit amidst risk across borders and continents."[6] The difference between the earlier and later phases was determined by technological development. Subsequent phases of globalisation and improved efficiency in the transactions sector generated flows of goods, bullion and labour that were far more extensive than ever before.

Another way of looking at the so-called phases of globalisation is to distinguish between early globalisms prior to the 16th century, and the globalisation of today. I have been reminded by Geraldine Heng, a scholar of literature and history, that "the more careful of contemporary cultural theorists do not usually deploy the term globalization mainly to indicate the planet's interconnectivity and networks."[7] While globalisation and globalism are terms that have been spoken about negatively and pitted against ideals like nationalism and awareness of local variation, their use in a scholarly context is helpful in thinking about the types of interconnectedness that Singapore has experienced. The term "early globalisms" can refer to the links between places and peoples around the world, even before the European maritime empires of the 16th to 19th centuries. She wrote that, "early globalisms" can be contrasted with contemporary globalisation, which is associated with "complex, often ironic, uneven and contradictory … outcomes produced by new

---

[6] Christopher Bayly, cited in Anthony G. Hopkins, "Introduction: Globalization — An Agenda for Historians," in *Globalization in World History* (London: Pimlico, 2002), 4.

[7] Geraldine Heng, Preface to "Whose Middle Ages?" (unpublished manuscript).

technologies" and "for which no premodern or early modern antecedents exist."[8] American political scientist Joseph Nye described globalism as a world system that is "characterised by networks of connections that span multi-continental distances." To him, globalisation refers to the degree to and speed with which globalism is expanding or declining.[9]

The dynamics that generated early globalism or the globalisation process were the networks that were established when migration of commodities, capital, ideas and people took place over long distances. From very early on, many parts of the world, especially those accessible by water, have been connected by long-distance trade, making possible the exchanges of goods, people and ideas. This was especially true of maritime Southeast Asia, which has been a region connected by commercial flows for centuries. As the axis between East Asia and the classical centres of India and the Middle East, and the focus of early modern maritime empires, the archipelagic seas have for centuries been shaped by trade and the global migration of peoples, cultures and religions.

Long before the Europeans arrived in Asia, trading communities from the Arab world to China flowed through and operated in the region. For instance, an extensive Arab trading network, stretching from the Persian Gulf to South China, was already in place from the middle of the 9th century. Traders from the South of the Arab peninsula were known to have plied the Indian Ocean routes, through Ceylon and the Nicobar Islands to the port of Kalah Bar (probably in modern Kedah in Malaysia) for trade. This extensive trade network also included Sumatra and Java, and extended eastwards through the Straits of Melaka, all the way to South China. It was through these connections that Islam first spread among the coastal cities, becoming the great religion of commerce throughout the Indian Ocean by the end of the 13th century.

Like the Arabs, Indian merchants from the Malabar and Coromandel

---

[8] Ibid.

[9] Joseph Nye, "Globalism Versus Globalization," *The Globalist*, 15 April 2002, https://www.theglobalist.com/globalism-versus-globalization/.

coasts had established trade links with Southeast Asia long before the arrival of the Europeans. They probably preceded the Arabs and the Chinese. Indeed, historians have claimed that, for more than two thousand years, "the lure of gold" had drawn Indian merchants to Southeast Asia.[10] By the 16th century, Indian traders were known to frequent the major trading emporia of Pegu, Ava, Tannasery, Kedah, and Melaka, where wares and produce were bought and sold.[11] Trade links were especially strong between South India and the Malay Peninsula, where the eastern Indian ports and their western Malayan counterparts served as important entrepôt centres in the East-West trade.

Chinese sailors and merchants were already a regular sight in Southeast Asia from the time of the Han Dynasty, acquiring fragrant timber, spices and other exotic goods in exchange for their Chinese pottery and silk. As a destination for trade, Southeast Asia then came to be known as part of the *Nanhai* (南海, denoting "Southern Sea") trading region.[12] The Nanhai region functioned as a trans-shipment hub for China's trade with the west as Chinese junks rarely travelled beyond the Straits of Melaka at that time. Indian and Ceylonese traders dominated the Indian Ocean leg of the Maritime Silk Road, while the Chinese dominated the Nanhai trade. Both groups would converge at the Malay Archipelago to trade.[13]

Southeast Asia grew in prominence during the Tang Dynasty period, when the Sumatra-based Srivijaya empire emerged as a dominant trading player along the Maritime Silk Road during the second half of the 7th century. There was direct contact between the Sumatran power and China around 670–680 CE, and Srivijaya was deemed important enough to receive a royal envoy in 683 CE. From the 8th century, Persian and Arab merchants operated the trading networks that connected the Chinese ports with the

---

[10] Kenneth McPherson, *The Indian Ocean: A History of People and the Sea* (Delhi: Oxford University Press, 1993), 55.

[11] Ibid., 59.

[12] Wang Gungwu, *The Nanhai Trade: The Early History of Chinese Trade in the South China Sea* (Singapore: Times Academic Press, 1998), 37.

[13] Ibid., 41.

Indian Ocean. With their involvement, maritime commercial activity during the Tang period included the export of silk, cloth, ceramics, tea, copper and iron wares from China to West Asia. The Tang-era shipwreck found in the Java sea — the Belitung Cargo — is evidence of this trade. Southeast Asia remained an important trading region throughout the Song Dynasty (Figure 4). During the Ming dynasty, notwithstanding changes in imperial policies on the conduct of trade, the Chinese maintained connections with many strategic ports in maritime Southeast Asia. The Zheng He voyages in the 15th century (1405–1433) marked the high point of Southeast Asia's connections with China, but even with the termination of the court-sanctioned expeditions, Chinese merchants continued to trade with the region.

Trading zones and maritime cities

By the 13th century, long distance East-West trade was conducted through an efficient segmentation of networks. These segments were the Arabian Seas, the Bay of Bengal and the South China Sea (Figure 5). These networks were underpinned by intermediate coastal stopovers, transit zones and trans-shipment points, which in turn developed into emporia where goods were collected, traded and distributed. Many eventually became maritime cities. Historian Anthony Reid points out that the build-up of trade networks led to a "great expansion of cities and ... gave them life."[14] He elaborates that in Southeast Asia, before 1630, "maritime cities were probably more dominant over their sparsely-populated hinterlands than they were in most other parts of the world."[15] Ayutthaya, Thăng Long (Hanoi), Banten, Aceh, Pegu and Melaka were examples of these maritime cities that developed into centres of wealth and power through trade, and later, colonial port cities.

Not surprisingly, relatively large populations of merchants and sailors

---

[14] Anthony Reid, "Economic and Social Change, c.1400–1800," in *The Cambridge History of Southeast Asia: Vol. 1, From Early Times to c. 1800, part 2*, ed. Nicholas Tarling (Cambridge: Cambridge University Press, 1992), 464.

[15] Ibid., 472.

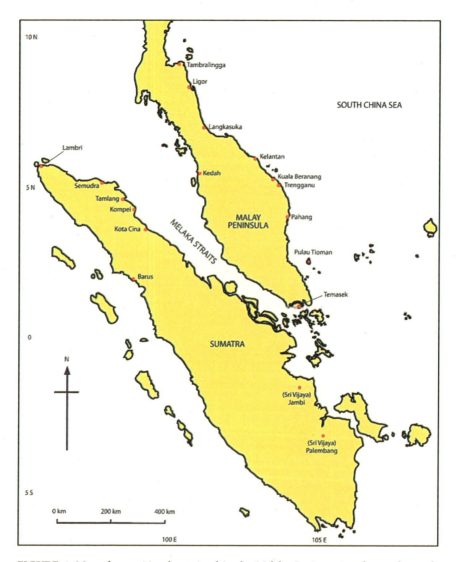

FIGURE 4: Map of port cities that existed in the Melaka Straits region during the tenth to fourteenth centuries. The location of the port settlements caused them to be orientated towards different major economic zones. Ports in the northern Straits region interacted primarily with the Indian Ocean market, while those in the southern Straits region interacted with the South China Sea and Java Sea markets. *Source:* Kwa Chong Guan, Derek Heng, & Tan Tai Yong, *Singapore: A 700 Year History* (Singapore: National Archives of Singapore, 2009), 22.

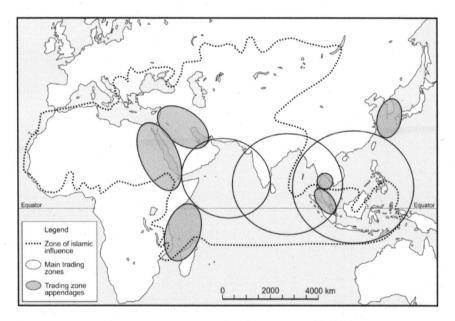

FIGURE 5: Map showing segmentation of trading zones in the early modern period. *Source:* © Peter Borschberg.

could be found in these maritime cities. Seasonal monsoon winds dictated the timing and regularity of travel along the shipping routes, limiting them to at most one return voyage per year. As a result, "Southeast Asian cities at their peak season are thronged with visiting traders from all over Asia."[16] In Melaka, for example, a large community of Tamil merchants, known locally as "klings", had settled with their families and were reported to have owned large estates and great ships. Many of these Tamil merchants went on to assume positions of power and authority in local society.[17] Similarly, Chinese communities settled where they traded, and from the 9th to the 15th centuries, travellers' accounts frequently noted the presence of settled Chinese communities in Palembang, Java, Cambodia, Siam and Melaka. Historian Wang Gungwu's concept of the Hokkien informal empire in the 15th century refers to traders from South China who were engaged in exchanges in the ports of Southeast Asia during that period.[18]

Colonial port city *par excellence*: Flows and circulations

Thus, prior to the colonial era, local merchants had preceded European trading companies in weaving together Asian webs of trade.[19] These webs were not broken up by colonial intervention; in fact, colonial trading structures built on these long existing practices. After Singapore was established as a trading colony by the British, it continued to function as a node of overlapping diasporic worlds and their networks. Colonialism in Singapore reinforced those systems and, by the end of the 19th century, the island became an established regional hub of an integrated system of trans-regional trade, pilgrimage and knowledge production. These functions, flows and networks sustained Singapore's strategic and economic position

[16] Ibid., 132.

[17] Kanakalatha Mukund, "Trade and Merchants: The Vijayanagar Period (1400–1600)," in *The Trading World of the Tamil Merchant: Evolution of Merchant Capitalism in the Coromandel* (Hyderabad: Orient Longman, 1999), 50.

[18] Loh Wei Leng with Jeffrey Seow, *Through Turbulent Terrain: Trade of the Straits Port of Penang* (Kuala Lumpur: Malaysian Branch of the Royal Asiatic Society, 2018), 16.

[19] Sunil S. Amrith, *Crossing the Bay of Bengal* (Cambridge, Massachusetts, and London, England: Harvard University Press, 2013), 35.

within the British empire, which, at the end of the 19th century, included Egypt, India, Jamaica, Nigeria, Burma, Malaya, Australia and New Zealand. Singapore was no longer a regional port-polity; as part of a global empire, it had integrated with an inter-continental world.

Nevertheless, as a colonial trading port, Singapore's trade was a predominantly Asian one, covering the Malay Archipelago, China and India. As trade grew in volume, the commercial networks that Singapore served shaped the form and structure of Singapore the port city and its plural society.[20]

Here is a literary re-imagination of a typical scene in Singapore from Amitav Ghosh's *River of Smoke*, which is set in the first half of the 19th century:

> *Well-heeled visitors to the island might prefer to do their shopping in the European and Chinese stores around Commercial Square, but for those of slender means and pinched purses — or those with no coins at all, but only fish and fowl to barter — this market, listed on no map and unknown to any municipality, was the place to go: for where else could a woman exchange a Khmer sampot for a Bilaan jacket? Where else could a fisherman trade a sarong for a coattee [sic], or a conical rain-hat for a Balinese cap? Where else could a man go, clothed in nothing but a loincloth, and walk away in a whalebone corset and silk slippers?[21]*

Singapore is depicted here as a site where assorted objects from elsewhere in Southeast Asia, or even the "distant corners of the Indian Ocean", could be obtained. Ghosh alludes to the dubious means through which some of the goods reached the *pakaian pasar*, or "clothes market", including violence, robbery and piracy. Still, the mind-boggling range of items available, and the market's "unusual kind of renown" far beyond

---

[20] Tan Tai Yong, "Port Cities and Hinterlands: A Comparative Study of Singapore and Calcutta," *Political Geography* 26, no. 7 (September 2007): 853.

[21] Amitav Ghosh, *River of Smoke* (New York: Farrar, Straus and Giroux, 2011), 108–9.

Singapore, showcased the free-wheeling laissez-faire attitude and mode of commercial exchange typical of port cities.

Raffles had boasted that, within three years of Singapore's founding, more than 3,000 vessels had called at Singapore's harbour.[22] Singapore's free port status attracted junks from Siam, Cambodia and Vietnam, which came to Singapore in droves. The arrival of these vessels brought goods and people, and led to "Singapore [having] one of the most diverse populations on earth."[23] As the port-city grew, so too did its migrant population. Numerous groups of people were drawn to Singapore for trade and for work. They arrived in different phases, but their numbers increased significantly with the opening of the Suez Canal in 1869 and advances in steamship technology. There was also an eight-fold increase in the volume of trade that passed through Singapore between 1873 and 1913 — a span of 40 years.[24]

A visitor to the bustling port city would have been struck by "the medley of peoples — Europeans, Chinese, Indian and native." This was an observation made by the British colonial administrator and scholar, John Sydenham Furnivall, who noted:

> *It is in the strictest sense a medley for they mix, but do not combine. Each group holds by its own religion, its own culture and language, its own ideas and ways. As individuals they meet, but only in the marketplace, in buying and selling. There is a plural society, with different sections of the community living side by side, but separately within the same political unit.*[25]

Furnivall, who was stationed in Burma for most of his career, argued that mass migration to colonial port cities in Southeast Asia resulted in

---

[22] Amrith, *Crossing the Bay of Bengal,* 70.

[23] Ibid.

[24] Mark R. Frost and Yu-Mei Balasingamchow, *Singapore: A Biography* (Singapore: Editions Didier Millet and National Museum of Singapore, 2012), 134.

[25] John Sydendam Furnivall, *Colonial Policy and Practice: A Comparative Study of Burma and Netherlands India* (Cambridge: Cambridge University Press, 1948), 304.

the creation of "plural societies". His thesis started to gain currency from the 1930s and 1940s onwards, and those who subscribe to this school of thought have pointed out that migrant communities worked and traded alongside one another in the marketplace, but they lived in ethnic enclaves, and their cultures remained closed and static. This segregation was further entrenched by municipal planning, which was shaped by three main considerations: "enabling business, anchoring the mercantile community, and segregating the different ethnic and occupational groups."[26]

Writing in 1934, Roland Braddell, a prominent lawyer, went to great lengths to describe the composition of different communities in Singapore. He categorised the Europeans, producing a long list of nationalities. He listed the Asian communities by ethnic group, detailing the many sub-groups under broader labels of "Malays", "Klings", "Asiatics" and "Chinese".[27] Singapore's economy was certainly very plural in terms of its participants and sources of exchange.

Populations of different race and religion coexisted, while living separately from one another. This could be seen from ethnic enclaves that developed based on the 1822 Town Plan that British colonial administrators had tried to implement (Figure 6). There was a designated European Town on the northern bank of the Singapore River, but European settlers subsequently moved away from the urbanising city centre, which was increasingly home to non-Caucasian communities.[28] By the middle of the

---

[26] Tan Tai Yong, "Port Cities and Hinterlands," 854.

[27] Lai Chee Kien, "Multi-Ethnic Enclaves Around Middle Road: An Examination of Early Urban Settlement in Singapore," *BiblioAsia*, July 2006. Roland Braddell's categorisation of the early composition of different communities in Singapore is summarised here:

- Europeans ("white people"): English, Irish, Scottish, Welsh, Australians, New Zealanders, Canadians, Americans, Belgians, Danes, Dutch, French, Germans, Greeks, Italians, Norwegians, Portuguese, Russians, Spaniards, Swedes, Swiss and others
- "Malays": "real" Malays, Javanese, Boyanese, Achinese, Bataks, Banjarese, Bugis, Dyaks, Menangkabau, people from Korinchi, Jambi, Palembang;
- "Klings": Tamils, Telugus, Malabaris; "Bengalis" include Punjabis, Sikhs, Bengalis, Hindustanis, Pathans, Gujeratis, Rajputs, Mahrattas, Parsees, Burmese and Gurkhas;
- "Asiatics": Arabs, Singhalese, Japanese, Annamites, Armenians, Filipinos, Oriental Jews, Persians, Siamese and others; "Chinese": Hok-kiens, Teo-chius, Khehs, Hok-Chias, Cantonese, Hailams, Hok-Chius, and Kwong-Sais.

[28] Ibid.

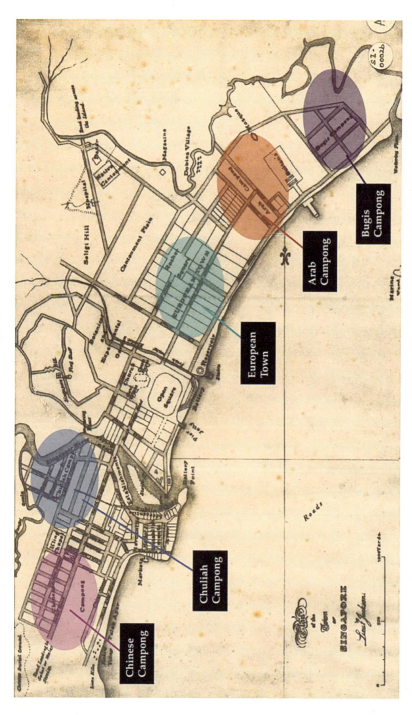

FIGURE 6: *Plan of the Town of Singapore* by Lieutenant Jackson, published in 1828, also known as the Raffles Town Plan. The different ethnic enclaves that developed based on the Plan have been separately indicated by Tan Tai Yong. *Source:* Collection of Singapore Land Authority, courtesy of National Archives of Singapore.

19th century, the port had become a kaleidoscope of different segregated communities, naturally coalescing along ethnic lines, and trading alongside one another in the marketplace. There were also more active measures of exclusion — colonial hotels tended to segregate non-white patrons without turning them away, by giving them differential treatment from European patrons.[29] While the port's business flew the flag of cosmopolitan openness, the social reality was at times one of strict boundaries between different groups that had converged on the city for trade and work.[30]

But, reality often defies neat categorisation, and Singapore was no exception. Historian Sunil S. Amrith has pointed out that "taking a broad view of migration, it is equally easy to find instances of cosmopolitanism and of segregation."[31] Singapore was not merely a location where different communities settled and coexisted side by side, more importantly, it was a site of complex interactions between diverse groups, facilitated by commerce, religious engagements and knowledge production.

Networks, circulations and new knowledge practices

This is where I would like to revisit the theme of flows and networks that sustained Singapore's strategic and economic position as a colonial port city. In my previous lecture, I referred to Tony Ballantyne's use of the metaphor of a web in his study of the British empire. Ballantyne's framework, which posits that "[the] British empire, as much as a spider's web, was dependent on inter-colonial exchanges" in capital, personnel and ideas,[32] allows historians to uncover flows and connections between colonies, which would otherwise go unnoticed when the focus is placed on individual colonies. Furthermore, "it underscores that the empire was a structure, a complex fabrication fashioned out of a great number

---

[29] Maurizio Peleggi, "The Social and Material Life of Colonial Hotels: Comfort Zones as Contact Zones in British Colombo and Singapore, ca. 1870–1930," *Journal of Social History* 46, no. 1 (2012): 141.

[30] Tan Tai Yong, "Port Cities and Hinterlands," 854.

[31] Sunil S. Amrith, *Migration and Diaspora in Modern Asia* (New York: Cambridge University Press, 2011), 11.

[32] Ballantyne, *Orientalism and Race*, 15.

of disparate parts [(colonies)] that were brought together into a variety of new relationships."[33]

I had spoken earlier about how colonial trading arrangements were essentially built on pre-existing networks that had been established by merchant communities. The colonial structures provided the conditions for older networks to be resuscitated and reinforced, and for new ones to emerge. The Asian rice trade, which stretched from China to the Straits and the Archipelago, and developed quite independently of the Europe-oriented trade zones, is a good example. By the mid-1800s, Singapore was, as historian Rajat Kanta Ray describes, "the centre of a dense web of Chinese finance and trade."[34]

A steady increase in Chinese migration to Singapore and Malaya, particularly among Chinese labourers, who found work in the plantations and mines, had led to a burgeoning demand for rice in the region. The lucrative trade in rice was dominated by Teochew rice merchants who were based in Singapore, but were also known as Siam traders because of the large rice mills they owned in Bangkok. Together with the Chinese rice millers in Saigon, the Teochew rice merchants controlled the largest disposable amount of rice in Southeast Asia. The most prominent among them was Choy Tsz Yong, who arrived in Singapore in the 1870s. Back in his native Swatow, Choy was a successful sugar merchant and a commission agent. Seeing an opportunity in the new trade in rice shipments, the Teochew merchant came to Singapore with a substantial amount of capital, which he proceeded to invest in the import of Chinese goods and in Siam rice. By 1908, Choy was the head of the local Teochew clan, and he owned four rice mills in Siam, which produced over 10 million dollars' worth of rice. Half of this rice was sent to Singapore, and the other half to Hong Kong.[35]

While we now have a sense of how commercial networks operated, what is less commonly known and researched are the new forms of

---

[33] Ballantyne, *Webs of Empire*, 45–46.

[34] Rajat Kanta Ray, "Asian Capital in the Age of European Domination: The Rise of the Bazaar, 1800–1914," *Modern Asian Studies* 29, No. 3 (July, 1995): 503.

[35] Ibid., 511–512.

knowledge and cultural adaptation that came about as the different migrant communities interacted with one another. How did practices and traditions change in the process of acculturation? Increasingly, historians are looking at colonial migration in terms of cultural exchanges that "produced creative instances of cultural hybridity."[36] For instance, in the absence of a common language and out of necessity, migrant communities developed new ways of communicating with one another and, in the process, created new linguistic and cultural forms.[37]

The *Huayi Tongyu* (华夷通语), which was published in Singapore in 1883, is a good example (Figure 7). The dictionary, or vocabulary book, to use a more accurate term, was one of several Chinese-Malay dictionaries produced in the 19th century as Chinese migration to Singapore and Malaya picked up significantly. Many of the migrants hailed from the Fujian and Guangdong provinces, and spoke Southern Min dialects such as Hokkien. In the absence of a common language, these Chinese migrants had initially found it hard to communicate and trade with the Malay-speaking local population. The dictionaries were a means for them to overcome the language barrier.

The *Huayi Tongyu* contains more than 2,800 words across 25 categories. The entries included common business phrases, names of food items, fruits, herbs, and household items, as well as terms and concepts used in subjects such as mathematics (numerals), geography and cosmology. The author of the dictionary also devised a rather ingenious method of phoneticising Malay words using southern Min dialects. Not only does the *Huayi Tongyu* provide a useful historical record of words that are obsolete or rarely used today, it also offers an insight into the lives of Chinese migrants and their interaction with the local population.[38]

The acquisition of linguistic skills gave certain merchant groups comparative advantage over others in the marketplace. However, not all

---

[36] Amrith, *Migration and Diaspora, 11.*

[37] Ibid.

[38] Lee Meiyu, "A Dictionary that Bridged Two Races," *BiblioAsia* 11, Issue 4, January 26, 2016, http://www.nlb.gov.sg/biblioasia/2016/01/26/a-dictionary-that-bridged-two-races/#sthash.pNEVuwEl.dpbs

FIGURE 7: Photograph of the *Huayi Tongyu* (华夷通语), published in Singapore in 1883, and an example of cultural exchange and hybridity. It was one of several Chinese-Malay dictionaries produced in the 19th century as Chinese migration to Singapore and Malaya picked up significantly. *Source:* National Library, Singapore.

merchant communities were equally adept at picking up languages. This was especially relevant before English emerged as the *lingua franca*. Making the case for more research on "knowledge practices", historian Claude Markovits argues that "contrary to what is often assumed, merchant skills are not a static body of recipes which are simply transmitted from one generation to another without any incremental aspect. Merchant knowledge is not purely routine but can often be innovative to a certain extent, at least inasmuch as it can adapt itself to changes in political and market conditions."[39]

One group that performed particularly well in this area were the Hyderabad Sindworkies, originally a monolingual Sindhi-speaking community. Unlike Jewish and Armenian merchants, who generally received a multilingual education from childhood, Sindhi merchants, who migrated in search of trade opportunities in the colonial period, had to acquire multiple business languages in a very short time. Markovits notes, "One is struck by the capacity of such merchant groups to process information into a body of knowledge, of a largely pragmatic kind, concerning markets, which gave them often an advantage over competitors and [which made them] actively sought out by others." He adds, "Thus in Southeast Asia, it was remarked that Japanese companies valued highly the knowledge about markets accumulated by their Sindhi agents, and that it was their possession of such knowledge that made the Sindhi (Hyderabadi) merchants indispensable intermediaries for some Japanese firms."[40]

Religious and commercial networks

There were other forms of networks built on ethnic and religious affinities that were effective because they fulfilled critical functions. Let me cite two examples to illustrate my point. The Nattukottai Chettiars had dominated the rural credit sector in many parts of Southeast Asia (Malaya, Burma,

---

[39] Claude Markovits, "Ethnicity, Locality and Circulation in Two Diasporic Merchant Networks from South Asia," in *The South Asian Diaspora: Transnational Networks and Changing Identities*, eds. Rajesh Rai and Peter Reeves (Abingdon, Oxon: Routledge, 2009), 21.

[40] Ibid.

Thailand and Cochinchina) in the 19th century. Chettiar financial activities had spanned the length and breadth of Southeast Asia even before the arrival of European colonialism; the increasing connectivity of the high noon of empire only served to strengthen the Chettiars' transnational financial network.[41] Chettiar temples were important nodes in this network, serving as clearing houses and places of business where Chettiar firms would congregate to transact with their clients. Furthermore, the temples provided a meeting place for the Chettiar Chamber of Commerce, allowing firms to exchange business information and set rules and norms governing the trade. Consequently, these temples facilitated the development of a cohesive network of social relations, bringing together the Chettiar community, allowing for the coordination of financial activities necessary for international financial operations.[42]

Religion played a central role in Chettiar moneylending. As devotees of Murugan, the Hindu god of war, Chettiar moneylenders would invoke the deity as chairman and witness to all economic transactions. Moreover, concentrated temple funds loaned to firms were seen as a means of drawing divine involvement into financial dealings. Considering the sacred connotations that moneylending had for the Chettiars, business ethics became imperative since unfair dealings would constitute sacrilege against their deity.[43]

It would appear that religion, with the symbolic testimony of a god, served as a means of guarantee for Chettiar business dealings and provided a unified, ethical code of conduct for business, in contrast to opportunistic behaviour among other merchant communities that operated across vast distances.[44] Thus, clients could expect a degree of

---

[41] Ummadevi Suppiah and Sivachandralingam Sundara Raja, *The Chettiar Role in Malaysia's Economic History* (Kuala Lumpur, Malaysia: University of Malaya Press, 2016), 6; Heiko Schrader, "Chettiar Finance in Colonial Asia," *Zeitschrift Für Ethnologie* 121, no. 1 (1996): 104–106.

[42] Schrader, "Chettiar Finance in Colonial Asia," 107–108; Hans-Dieter Evers and Jayarani Pavadarayan, *Asceticism and Ecstasy: The Chettiars of Singapore* (Bielefeld: Forschungsschwerpunkt Entwicklungssoziologie, Fakultat fur Soziologie, Universitat Bielefeld, 1980), 9, 11.

[43] Evers and Pavadarayan, *Asceticism and Ecstasy*, 11–12.

[44] Schrader, "Chettiar Finance in Colonial Asia," 107–108.

reliability and trustworthiness from Chettiars across Asia, facilitating international business. The Chettiars provided a ready source of credit for small businesses, which would otherwise have found it difficult to secure loans from European banks, and they counted Indian traders, Chinese miners and businessmen, European planters, Malay royalty and civil servants among their clients. In fact, it was known in Singapore and Malaysia that many a successful Chinese merchant had begun his climb with a loan from a Chettiar.[45]

My second example is the Haj pilgrimage trade. By the late 1800s, Singapore was the main departure point for Haj pilgrims who came from across Southeast Asia, especially the Malay-Indonesian region. Before embarking on their journey to Mecca, the pilgrims had to first travel from their hometown to Singapore. Bussorah Street in the Arab quarter was where Haj pilgrims could find many businesses that catered specifically to their needs, from clothing to accommodation.[46] In this setting, Malays from the region mingled with other Muslims of different social and economic backgrounds.

Arab communities played a key role in managing the pilgrimage markets. Prior to their arrival in Singapore, Arab merchants had successfully established commercial and social networks in the Indo-Malay Archipelago:

> *Using Singapore as a base, Arab recruiters roamed through the Malay-Indonesian communities seeking prospective pilgrims. Their task was to identify pilgrims, guide them through the preparatory process, and escort them to Arabia. Such was the degree of organization of such recruiters that they structured themselves into guilds and obtained recruiting licenses from the colonial authorities.*[47]

---

[45] K. S. Sandhu, "Indian Immigration and Settlement in Singapore," in *Indian Communities in Southeast Asia*, eds. K. S. Sandhu and A. Mani (Singapore: Institute of Southeast Asian Studies, 1993), 781–782.

[46] Frost and Balasingamchow, *Singapore: A Biography*, 103.

[47] Peter G. Riddell, "Arab Migrants and Islamization in the Malay World During the Colonial Period," *Indonesia and the Malay World* 29, no. 84 (2001): 124.

Given that the holy sites were in a foreign and distant land, Arab entrepreneurs in the Malay-Indonesian world served the function of promoting and facilitating participation from locals. For much of the last century of colonial rule, the pilgrimage trade was largely controlled by the Arabs in Singapore.[48] Arab-owned steamships transporting Haj pilgrims became a common sight at Singapore's harbour.

Although the pilgrimage trade started off small, it grew so rapidly that, by the end of the 19th century, the number of pilgrims had risen to more than 7,000 from a modest 2,000 pilgrims in the 1850s.[49] This number continued to increase, save for years during the First and Second World War. By the early 20th century, over 10,000 Malay-Indonesians embarked on the Haj annually.[50] After the introduction of air transport, the numbers ballooned, with over half a million Haj pilgrim passages in 1958 alone.[51] Throughout the years, the Haj remained an important driving force of migratory travels and mercantile trade.

Several factors were responsible for the growth of the pilgrimage trade in Southeast Asia. One significant factor — especially during the early periods — was the Arab communities in the region, who persuaded local Muslims to embark on the pilgrimage. In the 19th and 20th centuries, European companies also played a crucial role, introducing new technologies and organisational methods to the trade. For instance, steamship services and pilgrimage arrangement companies were introduced in the region, making mass transport by sea more accessible than before. European shipping companies also fostered networks with indigenous firms that provided access to markets, clients and cargoes. They incorporated these connections into the wider global networks they were assembling, creating larger economies of scale and efficiency in the pilgrimage trade.

---

[48] William R. Roff, "The Malayo-Muslim World of Singapore at the Close of the Nineteenth Century," *The Journal of Asian Studies* 24, no. 1 (1964): 80–81.

[49] Michael B. Miller, "Pilgrims' Progress: The Business of the Hajj," *Past & Present* 191, no. 1 (2006): 194.

[50] Ibid., 195.

[51] Ibid., 201.

Ultimately, the Haj was both a religious and commercial affair, and Singapore served as the locus for the pilgrimage trade in the region. It was profitable, but poorly regulated (especially in the early days), thus resulting in the exploitation of pilgrims. This was largely due to the British approach to the Haj, which oscillated between being motivated by profit and concern for their reputation as the governing power. Commercial interests ultimately won.

Given the extensive movement of Muslims through this affair, the Haj was a crucial factor in explaining migratory patterns and the formation of Malay communities in Singapore. It also led to the spread of ideas, customs and traditions. Malay-Indonesians returning from the Haj, for instance, were demonstrably more devout.[52]

Over time, the colonial rulers came to see these migratory movements as a threat, introducing social and political thought — often Islamic reformist ideas — from other regions. This was especially so with the Dutch, who initiated restrictive rules on Haj travels for the East Indies from the early 19th century. The British in Singapore, too, became concerned about Mecca as "the site for the spread of anti-colonial, pan-Islamic ideas during the haj season."[53]

Knowledge production

Colonial port cities, being diverse and metropolitan, provided public spheres where elites and literate classes socialised, discussed ideas and debated with one another. One such arena was provided by Malay publications such as newspapers, magazines and literature. The dissemination of these materials, and the accompanying spread of ideas, was stimulated by the advent of the Malay lithograph and subsequently the printing press, with the main distribution and publication centre situated in Singapore.[54] In fact, with

---

[52] Aiza Maslan, "Hajj and the Malayan Experience, 1860s–1941," *Kemanusiaan* 21, no. 2 (2014): 84.

[53] Nurfadzilah Yahaya, "Good Friends and Dangerous Enemies — British Images of the Arab Elite in Colonial Singapore (1819–1942)" (Master's dissertation, Department of History, National University of Singapore, 2006), 42.

[54] Roff, "The Malayo-Muslim World of Singapore," 84.

the "added stimulus of more frequent and intensive communication with the Middle East," coupled with the introduction of new communication technologies, Singapore quickly grew to become a centre for Islamic life, learning and literature in the Malay-Muslim world of the late 19th century.[55]

The printing press was introduced in Southeast Asia in the 16th century, with the first Malay book (a Malay-Dutch dictionary) published in Batavia in 1677. The first complete Malay Bible in Jawi was published in Batavia in 1746. Yet, it was only in the early 19th century that British missionaries set up stations and printing presses in Singapore to spread their religious ideas. The printing of Malay texts in Singapore had begun through a collaboration between Danish missionary Reverend Claudius Henry Thomsen and Abdullah bin Abdul Kadir, a translator from Melaka who is better known as Munshi Abdullah. The first printing press in Singapore, Mission Press, was established in 1823. Munshi Abdullah's original literary works, including the famous *Hikayat Abdullah*, were published by the press (Figure 8). Mission Press continued to be operated by missionaries, with the help of Munshi Abdullah as a translator, until the 1860s, when the "first indigenous printers and publishers emerged in Singapore."[56]

These indigenous printers were primarily immigrants from Java who had settled in Kampong Glam. The printing industry flourished from the 1860s, peaking in the 1880s. Early lithographic publications tended to be "jointly produced with contributions from copyists and owners of the text and press," resembling the form of a Malay manuscript.[57] Some of the most prolific Malay printers during the period included Haji Muhammad Said bin Haji Arsyad and Haji Muhammad Siraj bin Haji Salih. The former, along with his sons, published more than 200 Malay publications between 1873 and 1918, while the latter published more than 80 Malay books.[58]

---

[55] Ibid., 85.

[56] Mazelan Anuar, "Early Malay Printing in Singapore," *BiblioAsia*, 13, Issue 3, October 7, 2017, http://www.nlb.gov.sg/biblioasia/2017/10/07/early-malay-printing-in-singapore/.

[57] Ibid.

[58] Ibid.

FIGURE 8: Photograph of the *Hikayat Abdullah*, or *Stories of Abdullah,* one of the most important records of the socio-political landscape in Singapore, Melaka, Johor and Riau-Lingga at the turn of the 19th century. The *Hikayat Abdullah* was published by the first printing press in Singapore, Mission Press. *Source:* National Library, Singapore.

A key milestone in the early phases of the Malay vernacular press in the late 19th century was the publication of the first Malay newspaper in 1876, the *Jawi Peranakkan*.[59] The newspaper owned a significant number of lithograph presses, and had a circulation of approximately 250 copies.[60] In 1888, with the passing of the newspaper's chief editor, the *Jawi Peranakkan* struggled to keep afloat as public support diminished. During this period, another newspaper, *Sekolah Melayu*, emerged, aimed at catering to "the needs of students in Malay schools in Singapore."[61] *Sekolah Melayu* is significant in the history of the development of the Malay vernacular press as, for the first time, the "question of language was raised and discussed openly in the editorials."[62]

Indeed, similar to how new ideas on language emerged in the *Sekolah Melayu*, the increasing publication of Malay religious and secular writings in Singapore during the period helped to spread awareness of social and political thought, as well as expand the literary imagination of Malay Muslims in the Straits Settlements. Religious texts were a cornerstone of the publishing scene. In many parts of the world, printing has long been used to "diffuse religious and ethical literature."[63] In the early 1890s for instance, a *Wasiat* — literature on revivalist Islamic thought — circulated in profusion in the Straits, printed and reprinted in both Singapore and Palembang.[64] Other materials, such as "old and new translations of classical romances and legends of Arabic or Persian origin and Islamic flavour, traditional folk tales, poetry, and modern autobiographical chronicles" were also increasingly produced by Singapore lithographers.[65] Literary activity in the region was diversified and grew rapidly.

---

[59] Nik Ahmad Bin Haji Nik Hassan, "The Malay Press," *Journal of the Malayan Branch of the Royal Asiatic Society* 36, no. 1 (201) (May 1963): 38.

[60] Ernest W. Birch, "The Vernacular Press in the Straits," *Journal of the Straits Branch of the Royal Asiatic Society* 4 (December, 1879): 53.

[61] *Sekolah Melayu*, August 22, 1888.

[62] Nik Ahmad, "The Malay Press," 40.

[63] Hilary M. Carey, *Empires of Religion*, (Basingstoke: Palgrave Macmillan, 2008), 357.

[64] Roff, "The Malayo-Muslim World of Singapore," 84.

[65] Ibid.

After 1900, Malay lithographic printing output declined. Eventually, this printing technique was overtaken by the more efficient letterpress. Moreover, the Malay book market had to compete with publications from India and the Middle East, imported by Malay booksellers. Many local publishers were affected, and had to scale back on their output, eventually ceasing their operations. Nonetheless, while Malay lithographic printing became a lost art after the 1920s, Malay newspapers continued to garner a substantial audience. Newspapers became more popular with the increasing number of urban Malays because the "new medium was better able to fulfil the information needs of the community as well as adapt to their changing reading patterns."[66]

Religious questions only emerged from newspaper publications from 1906, with the establishment of the journal, *Al-Imam*.[67] After returning to Singapore from his studies in Egypt, *Al-Imam's* founder had a desire to "bring social and religious reforms into Malaya … purify Islam from malpractices and non-Islamic influences and to eradicate despondency, inertia and the feeling of inferiority which were predominant among the Muslims in Malaya."[68] While the paper only lasted three and a half years, its call for religious reforms were adopted by subsequent publications, such as the *Neracha*. The paper also enjoyed a responsive readership base, who wrote in to the paper to comment on their increased interest in Islam.[69]

It should also be noted that a diverse range of publications still existed during the period. The popular *Utusan Melayu*, for instance, focused largely on world news, and had no interest in dealing with religious issues. The first newspaper to be published daily, the *Lembaga Melayu* (1914–1931), also dealt mainly with foreign and domestic news, eventually becoming the main Malay language newspaper of the Straits Settlements until the 1930s, during which time Malayan political issues received prominent coverage.

---

[66] Mazelan Anuar, "Early Malay Printing in Singapore."

[67] Nik Ahmad, "The Malay Press," 44.

[68] Ibid., 45.

[69] Ibid.

Conclusion

Singapore was global in its outlook long before Rajaratnam articulated his vision of Singapore as a Global City. Singapore was home to flows of people and goods, and the site of networks sustained by commerce and religion. Amidst this context emerged hybridity, in terms of communities, cultural practices and ideas. For instance, Singapore was home to "mobile societies" such as the Southern Chinese trade diaspora, and creole communities like the Peranakans, who were the descendants of unions between mobile men from foreign lands and local women.[70] As Ho Engseng described it, Singapore was part of an inter-Asian space, crisscrossed by connections and societies.[71]

"Early globalisation" and the circulations, connections and networks had framed Singapore's port city existence. This interconnectivity took place at a pace slower than present-day instant communications, but was nonetheless very much present in pre-modern Singapore and its colonial days.

Finally, Singapore was both a plural and cosmopolitan city. What are the key features of plurality versus cosmopolitanism? A plural society, as described by Furnivall, is one that is segregated, with groups that live "side by side, yet without mingling."[72] According to Furnivall, different segments in a plural society would not share common values and social bonds. On the other hand, a cosmopolitan society is one where there is intermingling among different groups, and individuals look beyond national boundaries in building cultural, political and economic connections. Globalising cities tended to foster cosmopolitanism — an openness to divergent cultural experiences. At the same time, cities and their societies are fluid and

---

[70] There are the Peranakans, also known as Straits Chinese, whose origins are traced to intermarriages between Chinese traders and local Malay women in Penang, Melaka and Singapore, and the Jawi Peranakans, whose origins are traced to intermarriages between Tamil merchants and Malay women in Melaka.

[71] Ho Engseng, "Inter-Asian Concepts for Mobile Societies," *The Journal of Asian Studies* 76, no. 4 (November 2017): 907–28.

[72] James L. Peacock, "Plural Society in Southeast Asia," *The High School Journal* 56, no. 1 (1972): 1.

evolve over time. Singapore was at times more plural than cosmopolitan, sometimes both simultaneously.

We have good accounts of how specific diasporas came to settle in Singapore and adjusted to their new environment, but we know much less of how the different diasporas interacted with one another in daily life. Still, recent research has offered some insights into how print cultures and public institutions in the late colonial period facilitated cross-cultural interactions in Southeast Asian port cities.[73] Individuals' identities and affiliations were far more complex than broad categories could encapsulate. People came to Singapore, often just passing through, on their way to, or from, their intended destinations, yet settled down here. Indeed, Singapore became one of the most cosmopolitan cities in Asia by the end of the 19th century.

But where do we stand today? After decades of efforts in nation building and the promotion of racial harmony within the CMIO framework, do we risk developing a much more impoverished and narrow concept of what Singapore and Singaporeans are?[74] This is a question we ought to ponder as we attempt to strengthen our sense of identity. Even as we write and make our national history, we should take into account our much longer and richer past, where we were a point of

---

[73] Su Lin Lewis, *Cities in Motion: Urban Life and Cosmopolitanism in Southeast Asia, 1920–1940* (Cambridge: Cambridge University Press, 2016).

[74] CMIO refers to the categorisation of ethnic groups in Singapore by the government, as follows: Chinese, Malay, Indian and Others.

A recent Channel NewsAsia-IPS Survey on Ethnic Identity in Singapore found that more respondents reported that new citizens from Malay, Chinese, Indian or Eurasian backgrounds were more likely to be accepted as "truly Singaporean", compared to citizens from other backgrounds:

> At least three in five respondents reported that out of people from 10 backgrounds presented, those from any of them would be acceptable as "truly Singaporean" if they were to become new citizens. However, more respondents reported that new citizens from Malay, Chinese, Indian or Eurasian backgrounds would be accepted as "truly Singaporean". Although about 60% of respondents reported that citizens from Arab and African backgrounds would be accepted, this was relatively lower than the over 90% acceptance levels for those from Chinese, Malay and Indian backgrounds. This may potentially indicate that there is a close association between national identity, i.e., "Singaporeanness" and the core ethnic groups that have constituted it for decades.

See Mathew Mathews et al., "CNA-IPS Survey on Ethnic Identity in Singapore," *IPS Working Papers No. 28* (November 2017): 5.

convergence for people from all over the world — a place that afforded them opportunities, vitality, interactions and cross-cultural encounters, out of which grew a diverse, tolerant, multicultural population that went on to define modern Singapore.

Question-and-Answer Session
Moderated by Mr Kwa Chong Guan

Mr Kwa Chong Guan: Professor Tan has given us a very convincing account of Singapore's history as a port city. As he pointed out, a port city is a bit different from most other cities. A city is typically situated at a strategic location, where a settlement had developed because that was where a king had located his castle, peasants went for weekend markets, and pilgrims and travellers passed through. But a port city by definition started off as a harbour where sailors, mariners and traders stopped at the coast, and then a city grew around that port to service it. Singapore is no different from other colonial port cities, such as Chennai, which was a fishing village before it became a port, Calcutta, Banten in Java, or Jakarta. So, let me put the first question to Tai Yong — considering Singapore's historical trajectory from the 19th century to today, how did a global city come out of a port city? Going further back, the 19th century colonial port city had come out of, but was different from, the 14th century pre-colonial emporium that was Temasek, or arguably even the port under the Johor sultan in the Singapore River or the Kallang River estuary.

Prof. Tan Tai Yong: This is a big question. Let me try to answer it in two parts. In today's lecture, I was trying to highlight an instinct of Singapore that, for long parts of its history, it had functioned as an open entity that was connected to either the region or the rest of the world. Before 1819, it was connected to different trading networks at different times. After 1819, it was a colonial port city that did very well in terms of trade. Singapore was largely defined by its ability to stay open and connected, and to leverage opportunities offered by trading networks. But times changed and with the onset of technology, adaptation and innovation had to happen. You can see a transition from a port city to a global city as a strategic reaction, but the functions and approaches adopted by a port city and a global city are quite different.

Saskia Sassen has explained how global cities support multinational corporations through intermediation, where different cities create different types of specialisation. Port cities can remain port cities without becoming global cities, but in Singapore, the instinct and strategy have come together. Singapore is still a port city, but it is also a global city with a more complex set of operations.

Mr Kwa: Well, thank you, Tai Yong. Could I invite the first set of two or three questions?

Participant: You have pointed out the various continuities within Singapore and its past, but there are also discontinuities. An example of continuity is that we were a major trading centre then; we are a major trading centre now. An example of discontinuity — we were a major pilgrimage centre then; we are no longer a major pilgrimage centre now. So, if you had to compare Singapore of the last 50 years, with Singapore of the previous 600 years, for example, what are the major continuities that you see, and what are the major discontinuities, especially in the area of culture and identity?

Prof. Tan: In the 700-year history of Singapore, there are the continuities of Singapore needing to be cognisant of forces beyond its shores, and looking outwards for opportunities. Singapore's fate and fortunes have been determined to a large extent by external forces. That is a continuity, and so are trade, openness, and connectivity.

The largest discontinuity, in my view, is that in 1965, Singapore became a nation state. The stories that I have just told, which preceded 1965, were organic stories. The colonial state — the governing authority — was limited and laissez-faire. It was mainly concerned that money was made, and law and order maintained. There was no interest in developing society and looking after the welfare of people. People and communities looked after themselves. In 1965, we changed tack altogether — from a very limited state, we grew a very large state (in terms of governmental functions and interventions). Singapore became a developmental state, and in order to grow the economy and build a nation, the state participated in every aspect of life in the country. Therein lies the difference between a nation state and a city-state, which is a theme that I will get to in a subsequent lecture.

The point is that, if you look at Singapore's past, nation statehood has spanned only 53 years. It is a glitch in Singapore's 700-year history. But Singapore, as a successful port city from 1819 to 1965, was organically driven by people's energies, innovation and vitality. The state did not play much of a role, other than ensuring some degree of law and order, and, as I explained in the Haj example, the British were sometimes in two minds about regulation. So that is a fundamental difference. The question going forward is, what is the future of the nation state for Singapore?

Participant: I wonder if you would agree with me, that the 1920s were a very significant time: 1920 to 1930 was the first decade where births outnumbered deaths, and it was around the time when South China was becoming so unsafe that people were bringing their families to Singapore. In fact, over one doorway in Niven Road, there was a black board with gold lettering, and I was told that the writing on the board said, "We have brought our rice fields to the south," implying that they had given up hope of going back, and settled here. Wang Gungwu's wonderful biography also shows that the upper classes were trying to go back to China but were unable to. Until about 1920, we might say that Singapore had been a sort of major central business district in which people made a living, but intended to go back to their place of origin. But after this period, it became a place of families. Do you feel that this period was an important break in Singapore's history?

Prof. Tan: If you look at migration statistics, it is probably correct that from the 1870s, there was a lot of movement from South China to Singapore, but the precariousness of life here led to people not putting down roots in the island. However, from the 1920s, the colonial structure became a bit more established. This was when one started to see a settled, plural community — if you believe Furnivall — or a cosmopolitan society, developing in Singapore. Subsequently, there was the disruption of the war but following that, citizenship came into the picture, and Singapore's population became much more permanent.

Mr Kwa: Another key change was colonial policy. After 1910, a more welfare-oriented, "white man's burden" colonial policy was implemented, not only in Malaya, but also in the Dutch East Indies.

Participant: I have two related questions. The first is regarding Roland Braddell's description of the colonial constructions of race, which you mentioned in your lecture. Under the category of Malay racial groups, there were "real" Malays, and then a list of presumably "less real" Malays. Could you elaborate on how the colonial authorities understood the "real-ness" of Malays? The second question is, how far do you think these colonial constructions of race undergird today's conceptions of race in Singapore? Because it strikes me that the four groups resemble our present-day CMIO categories.

Prof. Tan: Racial categorisation in the colonies was a major preoccupation of the authorities because they needed this knowledge to govern. Many colonial practices in Singapore were derived from those in India, where the British authorities also categorised populations very carefully. This is not genetic science, and it was up to the colonial administrators to determine what were the distinguishing characteristics or features of different types of people. So, when they defined a "real" Malay, they probably had in mind certain criteria that needed to be met, if not, one would be considered "unsuitable" to be put into that category.

I am more familiar with the practices in India, so I will give you an example from India. The "martial race" in India was a category that the British developed to justify recruiting only from certain groups of people in India. The "martial race" was a colonial myth, created to justify why certain people would make better warriors than others.

You can say that there are environmental or geographical reasons why some people would more readily take up arms and fight than others. For instance, people in living in unsettled frontier lands might be more inclined to violence and fighting than people in an urban setting. But what is remarkable is that the British took these generalisations, developed them into an anthropology, and wrote books that detailed what a person belonging to this race would be like. People were classified based on their village, clan and ancestry, among others. They used this "colonial science" to separate and govern different groups, and this is probably what they did in Singapore. You saw from Roland Braddell's classification that they went to great detail in determining which group people belonged to. The British basically developed racial categories for census and other purposes, which Singapore inherited to some extent.

Participant: Given that Singapore has been an open entity reliant on the forces of globalisation for hundreds of years, how do we navigate a world that seems increasingly isolationist? Are there any historical examples that can help guide us today?

Prof. Tan: Yes, Singapore needs to be open to trade — our trade is more than three times our gross domestic product (GDP). An environment where states increasingly close their borders and move away from trading arrangements and trade pacts would be harmful for a trading nation like Singapore.

We need to be nimble. That is why I was talking about the instinct of Singapore, which is very different from the instinct of a large country that can just close its borders and turn inwards. To thrive, Singapore has no choice but to function as a hub and nodal point for connectivity.

This brings me back to my earlier point that Singapore is now both a city-state and a nation state, which has to confront the tension between being a nation state that needs to address the interests and concerns of its citizens, and being a city-state that thrives on being as open to the world as possible.

Participant: There have been discussions on China's Belt and Road Initiative providing funding for the Kra Isthmus Canal project in Thailand. Could Singapore maintain its position as a global city with regard to shipping and trading then, should the Kra Isthmus Canal plan be executed? There have also been reports of Chinese plans to invest in Malaysian and Indonesian ports.

Prof. Tan: The Isthmus of Kra has been talked about for several decades. The implication of cutting a canal across the Isthmus of Kra is that ships would not have to sail down so far south to Singapore, which could pose a threat to Singapore. We always speak of location — we are located at a point in the Straits of Melaka where ships have to sail through — as Singapore's fundamental advantage.

Indeed, some years ago, Malaysia tried to develop two ports in Pasir Gudang and Tanjung Pelepas, which are basically in our vicinity and could affect our strategic advantage. With the rise of airports in our region, our status as a transit air hub could also be affected.

Maintaining its geographic strategic advantage has historically been, and remains, a concern for Singapore. Singapore has to develop strategies to adapt to these changed circumstances and ride on and contend with the forces of globalisation, our good location notwithstanding.

Participant: From your presentation, it seemed like there were sizeable Arab, Persian, Armenian and Jewish communities in Singapore. Were there reasons for their decline to our present-day situation, or were they just not permanent residents of Singapore?

Prof. Tan: These communities are still present in Singapore — Armenians, Baghdadi Jews, and all. Our first Chief Minister David Marshall was one example. These communities have churches and other institutions here, but they are quite small. It looks like they have disappeared, but I think they still exist in small numbers. Furthermore, they are largely classified under the "Others" category. There have been lots of histories written on these small minority communities, and if you were to do some research, you would find that these groups of people who contributed to the making of modern Singapore have incredibly rich stories.

Participant: Was there a decline in their numbers from the earlier pre-colonial period?

Prof. Tan: There will be ups and downs as people move back, as birth rates drop, among other factors. But the numbers and corresponding changes in the communities are not large enough for us to determine a clear rise or decline.

An example is the Sikh population in Singapore. Sometimes they are not even captured by the census; they are just classified as Indians, so one does not really know the actual size of the population. When I was trying to write my undergraduate thesis on the Sikhs, there were census figures until 1950, and then after that, it was a "guesstimate". Members of the community would tell me that there are about 12,000 Sikhs in Singapore, and then you tried to estimate whether the population has increased or decreased over the years.

Participant: Until 1997, Hong Kong was pretty much laissez-faire, and the British governed it slightly differently from Singapore, because its society was more homogeneous, being mainly Southern Chinese. How might Singapore fare in the future, vis-à-vis Hong Kong? How will these two global cities compare?

Participant: When a country achieves some degree of prominence, they are able to offer some kind of contribution to the world. Take Switzerland, which is a safe haven for investments because it is regarded as inherently neutral. Or the United States, which has been able to uphold aspects of human rights.

Then there is Singapore and its rise to prominence as a logistical hub. When I look at Singapore, one of the major contributions it can offer to the world is how it has been able to have people of different races and religions come together in harmony, in a very peaceful society. That to me is quite wonderful. What I do not see enough of is Singapore's ability to export this to the rest of the world.

Prof. Tan: Let me start with the question about Hong Kong and Singapore. It is a big question, and there are many parts to it. I will simply say that Hong Kong is a Chinese city that currently exists under the "one country, two systems" principle, and its future will be determined by how it negotiates the two systems.

In contrast, Singapore is a sovereign nation state that decides its own future. Of course, its fortunes will be subjected to larger forces at work, but it is still a sovereign state. Singapore's hinterland, which I will discuss in my next lecture, has shifted over time, and the whole world now constitutes its hinterland. Hong Kong positions itself as a world city, but its Chinese hinterland is ultimately quite overwhelming, and will shape Hong Kong's destiny.

As for the second question, I think we want to make sure that Singapore's multicultural society will continue to flourish and evolve, but I do not know if it is the desire of Singapore's political leaders to present Singapore as an example to be adopted by the rest of the world. If others want to look at the Singapore example and see what lessons can be drawn from it, that is fine, but I do not think Singaporeans should prescribe Singapore as a model for the rest of the world.

These things will evolve. Just as you think that you have got it right, circumstances will change. Singapore is continually a work-in-progress. In fact, we could have a long debate about multiculturalism and whether we are really multicultural. But I understand the thrust of your question is, "What can Singapore offer to the world in terms of an example of governance?" and I think it has much to offer. I would advise you to go to the Lee Kuan Yew School of Public Policy, and find out more about how Singapore has done some things well, and adapted and adopted certain practices for its purposes.

The secret of Singapore's success is its ability to change and adapt to its circumstances. Singapore is not a static community, and here is where history is important. This is the essence of Singapore.

Mr Kwa: Tai Yong, you have raised many questions in your answers, and we ought to come back, and hopefully get more answers from your future lectures. On that note, I invite our audience to join me in thanking Tai Yong for his lecture.

Lecture III

SINGAPORE'S STORY
A Port City in Search of Hinterlands

Introduction

I have tried to situate Singapore's history in the larger context of regional and global dynamics in my first two lectures. I spoke of the continuities and disruptions in Singapore's past through cycles of historical developments and how Singapore was "global", long before the terms globalisation and global cities became topical.

In this narrative, Singapore's character, fortunes and evolution as a port city would appear to be critically determined by regional and global politics, trade and movements of people. Unlike a number of earlier prominent Asian colonial port cities that have faded into obscurity, Singapore has evolved and continues to function as a major metropolis. From a port city serving regional trading networks, Singapore has grown into a city-state whose economy, inextricably linked to an international system driven by commerce and enterprise, is sustained and nourished by global economic conditions. Historically, Singapore functioned as a port thriving on flows of people and trading networks that stretched from the Persian Gulf to the southern coast of China. Today, Singapore positions itself as a hub for the greater Asian region and beyond. And I would argue that the underlying plot of the Singapore story has not changed fundamentally throughout its history.

Singapore's rapid growth and status as a global city-state has attracted the attention of economists, sociologists and geographers. Interestingly, historians, preoccupied in the past with colonial and nationalist narratives, have yet to grapple with the processes and conditions that explain Singapore's progress from port to global city. A narrative of Singapore's development as port city thus offers an interesting case study. I am not suggesting that the traditional narratives of Singapore as colony and nation state are unimportant, but that studying Singapore as a port city is also key to understanding its identity. In doing so, we assign greater weight to external factors and global phenomena in the shaping of the economy and polity of Singapore. For instance, it considers how the character and personality of the island state might have roots in regional identities and dynamics that predate 1965 or even 1819. I shall address the following questions: What is a port city? What are its essential characteristics? And how was Singapore's historical development and personality linked to and influenced by its functions as a port city?

Port cities and hinterlands

Three key features of historical port cities are relevant for our analysis.

First, port cities are not merely "cities that happen to be on the shoreline"; they are economic entities whose character is maritime in nature.[1] Any serious consideration of the urban culture, personality and morphology of port cities would have to contend with their economic functions as nodes of sea-based trading networks. The port city is therefore a "place of contact where goods and people as well as cultures are transferred between land and maritime space."[2]

---

[1] Peter Reeves, Frank Broeze, and Kenneth McPherson, "Studying the Asian Port City," in *Brides of the Sea: Port Cities of Asia From the 16th to the 20th Centuries*, ed. Frank Broeze (Honolulu: University of Hawaii Press, 1989), 29–53.

[2] Atiya Habeeb Kidwai, "Conceptual and Methodological Issues: Ports, Port Cities and Port-Hinterlands," in *Ports and Their Hinterlands in India, 1700–1950*, ed. Indu Banga (New Delhi: Manohar Publications, 1992), 10.

When one considers the social, cultural and political connections within the port city, it is not difficult to see how its demographic and ethnic evolution is reflected in the city's economic functions. These functions in turn make the city cosmopolitan — in fact, require it to be so if it is to be successful. Scholars have pointed out that in port cities, "races, cultures and ideas as well as goods from a variety of places jostle, mix and enrich each other and the life of the city."[3] Port cities not only function as entrepôts for the movement of goods, labour and capital; they serve as nodal points for the reception and transmission of culture, knowledge and information.[4] Their functions in turn create opportunities and space for cultural mixing and hybridisation. Historical port cities that were polyglot centres include Batavia, Rangoon and Penang. Like Singapore, these port cities were home to different ethnic communities.

Second, port cities cannot exist without a hinterland. There are a few definitions of a hinterland, but I refer to a hinterland as the area that surrounds and serves a large city or port that depends on it for economic growth. Port cities are necessarily linked to hinterlands by trade, and serve as the conduit for the trade of the land to access the sea and markets beyond. There are different types of hinterlands. They include immediate hinterland (port area itself), primary hinterland (area where port and city assume a commanding role and determine the life of the area), commodity hinterland (based on shipment of particular types of commodities), and inferred hinterland (port's hegemony over a particular area, to the extent that it satisfies the demand for imports in the area it serves).[5]

In the 1970s and 1980s, the main preoccupation of studies on colonial port cities was the role they had played in colonial control in Asia.[6] These

---

[3] Rhoads Murphey, "On the Evolution of the Port City," in *Brides of the Sea: Port Cities of Asia From the 16th to the 20th Centuries*, ed. Frank Broeze (Honolulu: University of Hawaii Press, 1989), 225.

[4] Mark Frost, "'Wider Opportunities': Religious Revival, Nationalist Awakening and the Global Dimension in Colombo, 1870–1920," *Modern Asian Studies* 36, no. 4 (October 2002): 939.

[5] James Harold Bird, *Seaports and Seaport Terminals* (London: Hutchinson & Co, 1971).

[6] Dilip K. Basu, *The Rise and Growth of the Colonial Port Cities in Asia* (Berkeley: University Press of America, 1985).

studies revealed that colonial port cities often facilitated western influence, and that western trade systems and demands transformed the market hierarchies in colonial port cities, as well as the mercantile elites and communities of their hinterlands.

Port cities that function as entrepôts may not have specifically defined hinterlands of their own. Instead, their maritime space — or networks of seaborne links — often constituted their hinterlands. Singapore is a prime example. For extended periods of its history, the port-polity served as a trans-shipment centre whose development depended largely on its position and function in the trading networks in which it was situated. These trading networks were determined by a combination of geography and available modes of maritime transportation. In other words, Singapore's existence did not depend on a surrounding or nearby land mass. The main economic base that supported the small island's very existence was its maritime port. Singapore's hinterland was effectively the maritime space around it, which included much of the Southeast Asian archipelago.

Third, port functions have shaped the composition and social structure of port city populations, such as mercantile groups and their institutions, as well as the very milieu in which specific groups existed and operated.

It is evident that port cities are influenced to a large extent by the hinterlands.[7] How cities relate to their hinterlands often hint at the ways in which "global cities are formed, transformed and extended beyond their immediate geographical territoriality."[8] By focusing on how Singapore identified its hinterland, and how the hinterland had, in turn, influenced its development, a narrative could be developed to explain Singapore's evolution: for long periods in its history, as a port engaged in entrepôt trade, Singapore thrived without a clearly defined hinterland. It then found a land-based hinterland in the Malay peninsula in the late 19th century, only to lose it

---

[7] Kidwai, "Conceptual and Methodological Issues: Ports, Port Cities and Port-Hinterlands," 26.

[8] Kris Olds and Henry Yeung, "Pathways to Global City Formation: A View from the Developmental City-State of Singapore," *Review of International Political Economy* 11, no. 3 (June 1, 2004): 492.

in 1965. Singapore has continually defined and re-defined its hinterland. In essence, the underlying plot in this historical narrative is this: Singapore is a port city whose development and growth were tied to its functions within the respective regional and global networks in which it operated.

Singapore: Entrepôt trade and the Asian hinterland

Soon after the signing of the 1824 Anglo-Dutch Treaty, which confirmed Singapore's status as a British (East India Company) possession, its position as an important regional port and emporium began to grow. Trade within Southeast Asia accounted for nearly one-quarter of its overall volume of trade in the late 1820s. China accounted for about 23 per cent, and India 16 per cent.[9] The trade was essentially a maritime one; trade with mainland Southeast Asia accounted for just about 5 per cent.[10] Singapore's position between two oceans appeared to matter more than its overland connections at the southernmost tip of the Asian landmass. In fact, until 1923, when the Causeway was built, Singapore could be reached directly only by sea.

Located where it was, Singapore gathered for itself "the larger portion of the Archipelago trade in Malaysian hands" while Penang served "Burma, the west coast of the Malay Peninsula, part of the trade of Siam and Sumatra, especially [Acheh] and the west coast."[11] Singapore soon became "the great emporium and fulcrum" of the trade of the neighbouring seas, dealing mainly in local produce, known collectively as "Straits Produce" — the agricultural and mineral products grown or produced in the Malay archipelago and brought to the colonial ports for packing and shipment to consumer countries.[12] The nature of the trade and transactions gradually

---

[9] Wong Lin Ken, "The Trade of Singapore, 1819-69," *Journal of the Malayan Branch of the Royal Asiatic Society* 33, no. 4 (192) (1960): 4–315; Wong Lin Ken, "Singapore: Its Growth as an Entrepot Port, 1819-1941," *Journal of Southeast Asian Studies* 9, no. 1 (1978): 50–84.

[10] Wong Lin Ken, "Singapore: Its Growth as an Entrepot Port, 1819-1941," 50–84.

[11] Wong, "The Trade of Singapore," 73.

[12] George Bogaars, "The Effect of the Opening of the Suez Canal on the Trade and Development of Singapore," *Journal of the Malayan Branch of the Royal Asiatic Society* 28, no. 1 (169) (1955): 115.

incorporated the various islands of the East Indies, the Malay peninsula, Siam and parts of Indo-China.[13]

As such, Singapore's commercial hinterland was maritime-based, rather than land-based. The extent of Singapore's commercial hinterland was indicated by the origins of the vessels that arrived regularly at the port of Singapore to trade — from the Celebes, eastern Java, Gulf of Siam, Indo-China and the Malay peninsula (Figure 9).[14] Thus, in the early 19th century, the multitude of maritime vessels from around the region collectively determined the hinterland and the system of entrepôt trade in Singapore. The trading patterns were based on the intermeshing of a number of pre-existing networks that connected the Arab lands and India to the west and China to the east.

As trade grew in volume, the morphology of the port began to reflect its hinterlands. Different trading communities now gathered in the vicinity of the port and were physically separated into various sectors in the city. Its hinterlands not only provided the resources that sustained Singapore but supplied the human capital that eventually constituted the plural and cosmopolitan society of Singapore. As a port city that functioned as an emporium, it adopted an open immigration policy, enabling the easy movement of traders and workers who were key to its development. Overlapping hinterlands and networks created in the port city a "polyglot migrant world constituted by streams of immigrants from China, India, the Malay Archipelago, and other far-flung places."[15] It was during this period of growth as a colonial port city, when much older and indigenous transnational connections were revitalised, that Singapore became the heart of the intellectual world of Southeast Asia.

From the late 19th century onwards, the port city was not only

---

[13] Bogaars, "The Effect of the Opening of the Suez Canal," 117.

[14] Ibid., 118.

[15] Brenda Saw Ai Yeoh, "Changing Conceptions of Space in History Writing: A Selective Mapping of Writings on Singapore," in *At the Interstices and on the Margins: New Terrains in Southeast Asian History*, eds. Abu Talib Ahmad and Tan Liok Ee (Athens: Ohio University Press, 2003), 48.

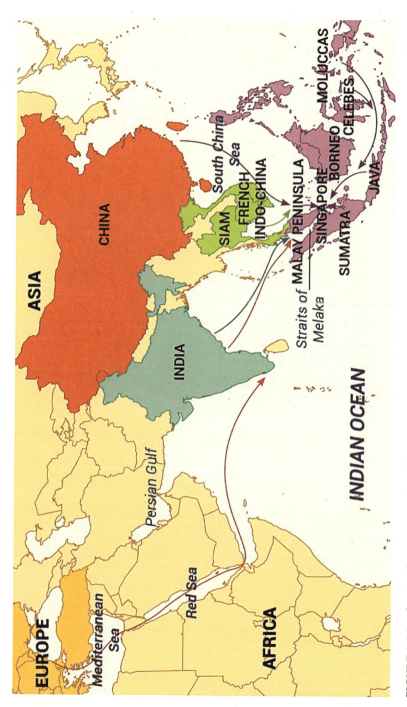

FIGURE 9: Map showing the movement of goods to Singapore. *Source: Singapore: The Making of A Nation-State, 1300–1975 (Secondary One)* (Singapore: Curriculum Planning & Development Division, Ministry of Education, Singapore; Star Publishing, 2014), 123.

bustling with commerce. It was a centre for Malay culture and literature, Chinese diasporic intellectual and political ferment, and Indian debates on cultural and religious reformism. As Singapore became the centre of overlapping migrant worlds, incorporating networks of trade, labour and cultures, it developed as a key economic and intellectual node in which "rich innovations in thought and behavior arose."[16] The port city became a centre of cultural and nationalist movements — a dynamic force for social change. It became what T. N. Harper calls a diasporic public sphere, where "information and ideas from outside lay in creative tension with an emerging local experience."[17] This experience was common in other colonial port cities like Rangoon and Penang, which were similarly home to hybrid communities that helped to shape a vibrant Asian public sphere.

Staple port and the Malayan hinterland

Until 1874, when the British began extending political control over the Malay States, Singapore did not have a clearly defined and formal hinterland that was under British administration. The bulk of its hinterland had been constituted by the Dutch East Indies — current-day Indonesia — and, to some extent, South China.[18]

By the late 19th century, Singapore's hinterland became more clearly defined. It served as a staple port to the Malay peninsula. During this period, the traditional idea of the hinterland supplying its cities was turned on its head as Singapore played the role of supplier through its exports to the Malayan hinterland and the Dutch East Indies. Singapore became the conduit through which food supplies from Siam, Burma and Indo-China were re-directed to workers in the Malayan and Dutch East Indies export industries. Economic historian Gregg Huff points out that "the dominant

---

[16] T.N. Harper, "Lim Chin Siong and the 'Singapore Story'," in *Comet In Our Sky: Lim Chin Siong In History*, eds. Tan Jing Quee and Jomo K. S. (Kuala Lumpur: INSAN, 2001), 7.

[17] Ibid.

[18] Wong Lin Ken, "Commercial Growth Before the Second World War," in *A History of Singapore*, eds. Ernest C.T. Chew and Edwin Lee (Singapore: Oxford University Press, 1991), 48–52.

feature of Singapore's exports of food and manufactures to [Southeast Asia] was the size of the [Dutch East Indies] market, which was twice that of the Malay peninsula (excluding inter-port trade)."[19]

As staple port to the Malay peninsula, Singapore was where tin, rubber and petroleum extracted from the peninsula were processed and exported to the rest of the world. The links between Singapore and its hinterland were very clearly defined and took on several forms. First, there were comprehensive transport links that connected the various mines in western Malaya to Singapore. The rail and road networks that developed with the rise of the tin and rubber industries integrated the island fully with its northern hinterland. Besides transport links, the integration of Singapore with its northern hinterland was facilitated by the integrated economy that revolved around tin and rubber. There was a complex system of trade and credit incorporating European merchant houses, Asian dealers and local retailers in Singapore. By the final quarter of the 19th century, the processing and export of staple produce from the Malayan hinterland had become a mainstay of Singapore's port-driven economy:

> In 1864, 291 tons of tin reached Singapore from the Malay states: six years later, the imports amounted to 4,025 tons, and by 1879 they had risen to 5,283 tons .... In 1817, 417 coasting vessels reached Singapore from both sides of the peninsula: by 1878 the total for the year had risen to 1,798 vessels and in 1879 it amounted to 2,569 vessels, more than six times the numbers arriving eight years earlier.[20]

Singapore's exports of tin would continue to grow, as seen from how, by 1899, tin accounted for nearly a fifth of the value of Singapore's exports. Singapore was also the world's main tin exporter at this time. Similarly, by

---

[19] W. G. Huff, "Singapore in the Late Nineteenth Century," in *The Economic Growth of Singapore: Trade and Development in the Twentieth Century* (Cambridge: Cambridge University Press, 1994), 54.

[20] Bogaars, "The Effect of the Opening of the Suez Canal," 120.

1918, the rubber auctioned in Singapore amounted to nearly a quarter of the world's exports. The large quantities of Malayan tin and rubber that made their way through Singapore's market stimulated its economy and paved the way for the construction of port facilities that were unrivalled in the region. It also prompted the establishment of a government port trust, known as Singapore Harbour Board from 1913, which eventually became the Port of Singapore Authority.[21] Singapore would continue to expand its volume of trade over the years.

Hinterland found and lost

By the beginning of the 20th century, Singapore was an integral part of the Malay peninsula, serving as its primary staple port. It was also developed as an imperial naval base in the 1920s. And notwithstanding the persistent myth of the Singapore guns facing the wrong direction, British military planners had incorporated the peninsula as part of the defence sector of the naval base in Singapore. This close port-hinterland relationship was thought to be a natural one, but it was soon torn apart by imperial policymakers in London.

In the midst of World War II, planners in London began drawing strategies for the post-war development of Malaya and Singapore. The Malayan Union Plan, which was hatched in 1944, envisaged a separation of Malaya and Singapore. Adopted and implemented in 1946, the Plan saw an amalgamation of the Malay States, in which Singapore, with its predominantly Chinese population, did not seem to fit. The Plan did not last, and was scuttled by determined opposition from a nascent Malay nationalist movement that opposed the Plan's liberal citizenship rules and the political emasculation of the sultans. It was replaced by the Federation scheme, which addressed many of the concerns raised by the Plan's opponents. But this did not change the position of Singapore. Separation, much to the chagrin of the local leaders of Singapore, seemed permanent.

---

[21] Lee Soo Ann, *Singapore: From Place to Nation*, 4th ed. (Pearson Education South Asia, 2019), 39, 47–51.

Hopes were harboured that Singapore would return to the Malayan fold. The staple port had become so used to its hinterland that it had become inconceivable that Singapore could survive without it. This was an interesting case of historical amnesia, as Singapore had earlier thrived without relying primarily on that physical hinterland.

In any case, even as political developments in Singapore and Malaya began to take off on separate trajectories after 1947, the aim of Singapore's political leadership was to merge the port city and its northern hinterland. From 1948, Singapore leaders from a range of political parties argued that political separation was an anomaly. The island's first two elected chief ministers, David Marshall and Lim Yew Hock of the Labour Front government, made repeated overtures to the Malayan Prime Minister, Tunku Abdul Rahman, urging him to consider merger with Singapore. The Malayan leader chose, however, not to reciprocate, uncertain if the conditions were right, where Malayan interests were concerned, to consider bringing Singapore into the Malayan fold.

It was only through the determined pursuit of Lee Kuan Yew and his People's Action Party (PAP) after 1959 that Merger between Singapore and the Federation of Malaya became a reality. Among the platforms upon which the PAP campaigned in the 1959 elections was the pledge to bring Singapore into a united Malaya. From its inception in November 1954, the PAP had declared ending colonialism in Singapore as one of its main objectives. This would be done through the establishment of an "independent [and non-communist] national state of Malaya comprising the ... Federation of Malaya and the Colony of Singapore."[22]

The PAP built their case on economics — the need to create out of the Malayan hinterland a common market that would sustain and nurture Singapore's attempts at industrialisation. Throughout the 1950s, the island colony had been under mounting economic pressure due to its explosive rate of population growth and declining entrepôt trade. Its re-exports to

---

[22] National Archives, United Kingdom, "Relations between Federation of Malaya and Singapore, 1960–1961," CO 1030/973: FED 59/03/01 Part B, https://discovery.nationalarchives.gov.uk/details/r/C338936.

the region had been dramatically reduced, owing to import restrictions on the part of many of its neighbours to protect their own nascent industries. Entrepôt trade — the mainstay of the Singapore economy — was also threatened by countries increasingly engaged in direct trading.

Another problem that the PAP argued could be alleviated with Merger was the lack of employment opportunities. For Singapore to provide enough jobs for its young and fast growing population as well as reduce its dependence on entrepôt trade, it would have to embark on a course of rapid industrialisation. But, for this to work, integration with the economy and markets of the Federation was crucial.[23] Then Finance Minister Goh Keng Swee asserted that, "whatever we do, major changes in our economy are only possible if Singapore and the Federation are integrated as one economy."[24]

There were also political reasons for Merger. There was a fierce tussle for power between a well-organised left-wing group and the faction led by Lee Kuan Yew. The successful conclusion of Merger, leading to the end of colonial rule, would take the wind out of the sails of the left-wing movement, and the anti-communist British and Malayan authorities would become staunch allies in Lee's fight against his left-wing and pro-communist rivals.

But Singapore's case for Merger was built on the need for a clearly defined and functioning hinterland that would continue to support its port economy. Without some form of economic integration or common market, the Singapore and Malayan economies would find themselves in direct competition with each other, particularly in attracting foreign investors. Singapore, with its smaller workforce and higher production costs, found that it was in a disadvantageous position as many local companies, such as small rubber footwear firms, were moving out of Singapore into the Federation, where costs of production were much lower.

---

[23] This was articulated by Lee Kuan Yew at the luncheon of the Singapore Union of Journalists, May 24, 1963, http://www.nas.gov.sg/archivesonline/data/pdfdoc/lky19630524.pdf.

[24] Goh Keng Swee, cited in Constance Mary Turnbull, *A History of Singapore, 1819–1988*, 2nd ed. (Singapore: Oxford University Press, 1989), 267.

Complicating matters was Singapore's status as a free port. Companies operating in Singapore could not rely on tariff protection for their goods, unlike those operating in other states in the Federation.[25] Without the hinterland and a common market, Singapore was therefore faced with a double whammy: it could not protect its local industries by imposing tariffs on foreign competition, and its manufactured products would not easily find their way into Malayan markets because of the Federation's tariff barrier.

Singapore regained her northern hinterland when it formed Malaysia with the Federation of Malaya, Sabah and Sarawak in 1963. But this proved to be short-lived. In August 1965, following two stormy years in Malaysia, Singapore separated from the Federation. Political differences proved insurmountable and, once again, a new hinterland had to be found.

After Separation and since independence, Singapore has continued to define and re-define its hinterland. As I pointed out in my previous lecture, in 1972, then Foreign Minister S Rajaratnam had challenged Singapore to aspire towards global city status, making the world its hinterland. More recently, in 2001, then Prime Minister Goh Chok Tong spoke of a seven-hour hinterland, encompassing a region within seven-hour flight radius from Singapore (Figure 10). He highlighted China and India as new markets within this hinterland. In 2001, this hinterland included 2.8 billion people living in various countries and cities, with hundreds of millions in the middle income group.[26] Subsequently, in 2004, Prime Minister Lee Hsien Loong also made mention of this seven-hour hinterland, referring to major markets such as ASEAN, China, India, Japan, Korea and Australia.[27]

---

[25] National Archives, United Kingdom, "Relations between Federation of Malaya and Singapore, 1959–1960," CO 1030/972, FED 59/03/01 Part A, https://discovery.nationalarchives.gov.uk/details/r/C338935.

[26] Ministry of Information and the Arts, "PM Goh Chok Tong's National Day Rally 2001 Speech, 19 Aug 2001," National Archives of Singapore, August 19, 2001, http://www.nas.gov.sg/archivesonline/speeches/view-html?filename=2001081903.htm.

[27] Ministry of Information, Communications and the Arts, "Speech by Mr Lee Hsien Loong, Prime Minister and Minister for Finance, at the Opening of Global Entrepolis @ Singapore 2004," National Archives of Singapore, October 11, 2004, http://www.nas.gov.sg/archivesonline/speeches/view-html?filename=2004101192.htm.

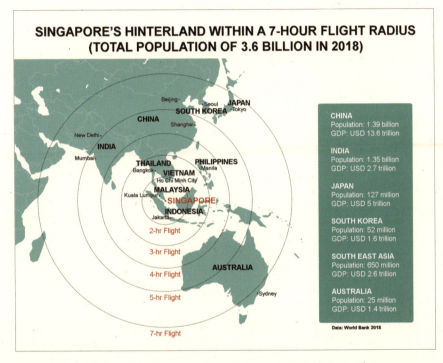

FIGURE 10: Graphic showing region within a seven-hour flight radius of Singapore. Data from World Bank (2018). *Source:* Cai Dewei, for the Institute of Policy Studies.

Singapore's relationship with Malaysia today illustrates this economic reality amply. While a common market was not achieved when Singapore was in Malaysia, our northern neighbour remains a hinterland of sorts as Malaysia is Singapore's second largest trading partner after China, with total bilateral trade amounting to S$93.8 billion in 2016.[28] Malaysia's trade with Singapore accounted for 13 per cent of its total trade, only topped by Malaysia's trade with China, which made up 15.8 per cent of its total trade.[29] The colonial masters are long gone and we are more than 50 years from Separation, but the economic, cultural, and personal ties remain, realised through old and new networks, physical and virtual.

Changing nature of hinterlands

Has the decline in relative importance of the Malayan hinterland for Singapore affected the evolution of Singapore from colonial port city to global city-state? Not much. For Singapore, the shifting circumstances in which economic space was constantly being re-defined meant that hinterlands were not fixed entities and were regularly being constructed. From the 14th century to the late 19th century, its hinterland was the regional maritime space before Malaya became the obvious proximate, physical economic hinterland (Figure 11).

For a global city in a globalised world, the notion of a fixed economic hinterland seems manifestly anachronistic. Singapore does not primarily serve peninsular Malaysia in a foreland-hinterland relationship, but depends more on its role as a hub port in global shipping networks. In fact, Singapore now faces competition from its former hinterland, in the form of Malaysian ports located close by, such as the Port of Tanjung Pelepas and Johor Port.[30]

---

[28] Enterprise Singapore, "Malaysia: Market Profile," last updated on February 26, 2019, https://www.enterprisesg.gov.sg/overseas-markets/asia-pacific/Malaysia/market-profile

[29] Kementerian Kewangan Malaysia, "Malaysia's Trade with Major Trading Partners," 2017, http://www.treasury.gov.my/pdf/economy/er/1617/st3_1.pdf

[30] Sharon Siddique, *Asian Port Cities: Uniting Land and Water Worlds* (Singapore: Lee Kuan Yew Centre for Innovative Cities, 2016), 52.

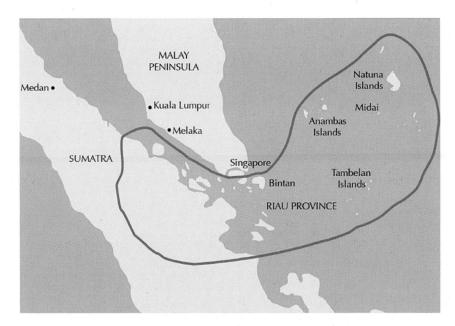

FIGURE 11: Map of the Riau-Lingga Archipelago and Natuna Islands. It is likely that this archipelagic area was part of Temasek's economic sphere. *Source:* Kwa Chong Guan, Derek Heng, Peter Borschberg, & Tan Tai Yong, *Seven Hundred Years: A History of Singapore* (Singapore: National Library Board and Marshall Cavendish, 2019), 45.

There is no question that trade will remain the lifeblood of Singapore. From regional emporium to nation state, Singapore has remained at its core an economic entity, totally dedicated to its regional and international outward-looking vocation of trade and commerce. Singapore continues to rely on exports, including machinery and transport equipment, chemicals and chemical products and manufactured goods.[31] From a traditional entrepôt port city, Singapore has metamorphosed into a global city-state. Its role as the middleman in regional trade may have eroded in the 1970s with the emerging economic nationalism of neighbouring countries, but its enduring entrepôt instinct remains. This is perhaps best summed up in the following remarks, made by then Minister for Trade and Industry George Yeo in 2000:

> In Singapore, you buy cheapest and sell dearest. We do not grow coffee in Singapore, yet we are a major supplier of coffee beans in the world. We produce no spices, but we are the centre of the Southeast Asian spice trade. We are also the biggest exporter of Swiss watches in the region. We have no oil, but we refine a lot of it and we are the trading centre for oil and other related products. Singapore's trade is 2.5 times its GNP.[32]

Today, Singapore's trade is more than three times its gross domestic product (GDP) — the highest trade to GDP ratio in the world. The operations may be more sophisticated, the materials dealt with different, and the scope much wider, but at the heart of its thriving economy lies a great port through which goods still find their way to regional and international markets.

Furthermore, as Yeo put it, "we are moving from seaport to airport to teleport" but embracing all three.[33] This can be seen from Changi Airport's

[31] Singapore Department of Statistics, "Singapore International Trade," Statistics Singapore —Singapore International Trade, 2019, http://www.singstat.gov.sg/modules/infographics/singapore-international-trade.

[32] George Yeo, "Speech on Information Technology and Singapore's Future," (keynote address at EMASIA, Los Angeles, June 4, 1998), National Archives of Singapore, http://www.nas.gov.sg/archivesonline/speeches/view-html?filename= 1998060502.htm

[33] John Curtis Perry, Singapore: Unlikely Power (New York: Oxford University Press, 2017), 259.

continued expansion, and the ongoing construction of Tuas Port. Tuas Port will consolidate Singapore's port operations and handle up to 65 million twenty-foot equivalent units (TEU) when fully operational, an increase from the Port of Singapore's existing capacity of 50 million TEU.[34] The port continues to shape the fortunes of the country. In 2017, Singapore was the second busiest container port in the world after Shanghai, handling over 33.6 million TEU (Figure 12),[35] and the world's busiest port in terms of overall shipping tonnage, with more than 130,000 vessel calls annually.[36] In 2012, 2015 and 2017, it was ranked alongside cities such as Hamburg, London, Oslo and Shanghai as a leading maritime capital globally, based on categories like shipping, ports and logistics and maritime technology, by Norwegian consulting firm Menon Economics.[37] Singapore's pursuit of Free Trade Agreements (FTAs) with partners worldwide underscores the role that international trade has played in the evolution of Singapore, and the vital importance of a global hinterland for its survival.

The future of port cities

In this lecture, I have examined how the dynamics generated by a port city in search of hinterlands have shaped Singapore's history. I first argue that Singapore had a fluid hinterland. Its economic, social and cultural hinterlands were defined by maritime trade that it conducted and the networks that were developed as a result of its commercial activities. As a result, its evolution and outlook are cosmopolitan and its identity an ongoing state of culture mixing. In this respect, Hong Kong offers an interesting comparison. Throughout its evolution as a port city, Hong Kong has had a clearly defined and dominant hinterland — China.

---

[34] David Kim Hin Ho and Ho Mun Wai, *Singapore Chronicles: Gateways* (Singapore: Straits Times Press, 2016).

[35] Hong Kong Marine Department, "Ranking of Container Ports of the World," April 2018, https://www.mardep.gov.hk/en/publication/pdf/portstat_2_y_b5.pdf.

[36] Maritime and Port Authority of Singapore, "Introduction to Maritime Singapore: Premier Global Hub Port," Maritime Singapore, 20 November 2017, https://www.mpa.gov.sg/web/portal/home/maritime-singapore/introduction-to-maritime-singapore/premier-hub-port.

[37] Erik W Jakobsen et al., "The Leading Maritime Capitals of the World 2017" (Menon Economics, 2017).

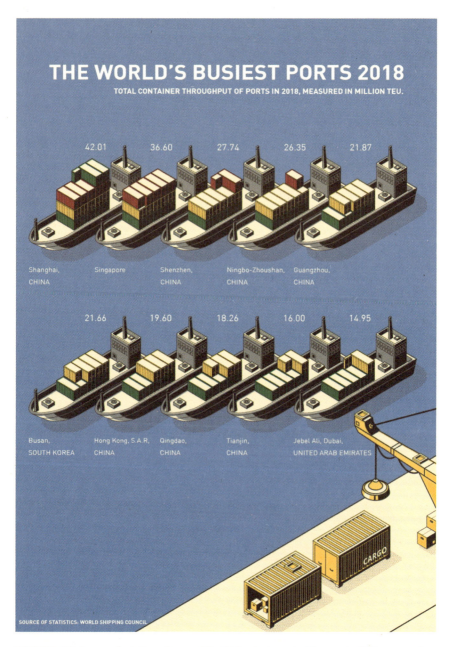

FIGURE 12: Image depicting the world's 10 busiest ports. The port of Singapore has consistently ranked among the top 10. Based on statistics from 2014 to 2018, it has been the world's second busiest port. *Source:* Cai Dewei, for the Institute of Policy Studies.

With the handover of Hong Kong from Britain to China, Hong Kong increasingly shares in the strengths and weaknesses of China's conditions and institutions.[38] For instance, Hong Kong's approach to port governance is likely to become more focused due to competition from Shanghai and Shenzhen. The establishment of the Hong Kong Maritime and Port Board in 2016 marks a shift from its earlier laissez-faire style of economic governance, linked to its history as a British colony with little government intervention.[39] While Hong Kong retains its cosmopolitan reputation, it is being re-absorbed into its hinterland in a process that began with its return to China in 1997.

I have tried to demonstrate that hinterlands are not always fixed entities and that port cities engaged in entrepôt trade often have to contend with shifting and sometimes overlapping hinterlands. The challenge here, for scholars especially, is to have conceptual clarity about the multifaceted nature of hinterlands, not only in spatial terms but in functional meanings as well. Is the relationship determined by functions or processes? Do hinterlands still have meaning in a globalised world? In the case of Singapore, it may be useful to ask if hinterlands locate their port cities, or vice versa. Is the story of Singapore after 1965 one of a continued search for or creation of some form of hinterland? Singapore's still expanding network of FTAs reflects this preoccupation with expanding the city-state's economic space.

Finally, I want to ask how port cities cease being port cities. Many important port cities in history have fallen by the wayside, "bypassed by most of their former enriching flow of exchange and hybridization."[40]

---

[38] See *Report of the Commission appointed by the Governor of Hong Kong to enquire into the causes and effects of the present trade depression in Hong Kong and make recommendations for the amelioration of the existing position and for the improvement of the trade of the Colony (1935) Hong Kong* (Hong Kong: Noronha & Co., 1935), 71, https://catalogue.nla.gov.au/Record/2939499.

[39] Sharon Siddique, "Port Governance," in *Asian Port Cities: Uniting Land and Water Worlds* (Singapore: Lee Kuan Yew Centre for Innovative Cities, 2016), 65–69.

[40] Tan Tai Yong, "Singapore's Story: A Port City in Search of Hinterlands," in *Port Cities in Asia and Europe*, eds. Arndt Graf and Chua Beng Huat (Abingdon, Oxon: Taylor and Francis, 2009), 217.

Calcutta is one such example. Formerly the capital of British India, it had all the characteristics of a thriving port city. However, from 1912, the British shifted the capital to New Delhi. The partition of Bengal in 1947 proved to be a major setback to Calcutta. An influx of refugees into the city put considerable strain on its resources and led to severe overcrowding. Furthermore, Calcutta's trade had been dominated by an inland commercial hinterland — but the partition of the province deprived the port of at least 30 per cent of its primary hinterland.[41] Today, Calcutta is a large regional city, and some regard it as India's cultural capital, but it has declined in economic strength. The vulnerability of port cities can be seen in how quickly they rise and fall. Shanghai has rapidly risen to be the world's leading port. On the other hand, New York's port has shrunk, and the city has lost its maritime functions in the city centre, which were shifted to its new container port on the other side of the Hudson River. London, formerly one of the most important maritime hubs in the world, is no longer a major world port.[42]

At the same time, some ports have developed into the biggest cities in the world today. Their traditional port functions have been eclipsed by their other roles as manufacturing, financial, service, and administrative centres, allowing them to retain their dynamism and cosmopolitanism previously tied to their port city status. London and New York are prominent examples of port cities turned global cities with diverse functions. In particular, London's riverine port has struggled to remain commercially viable in light of innovations like the bulk carrier and container. However, London continues to thrive as a global financial centre, being the top market for bonds and currencies, and hosting the most number of foreign banks of any financial centre. London also leads the world in terms of areas of expertise like maritime law, journalism and intelligence, continuing to retain and attract human capital.[43]

---

[41] Tan Tai Yong, "Port Cities and Hinterlands," 859–61.

[42] Perry, *Singapore: Unlikely Power*, 259; Carola Hein, *Port Cities: Dynamic Landscapes and Global Networks* (London and New York: Routledge, 2011), 51.

[43] Perry, *Singapore: Unlikely Power*, 260.

Some studies have referred to "world maritime cities", where container shipping companies and container terminal operators are present, as well as linkages to the world maritime market.[44] Singapore has transformed into one of these world maritime cities — it opened its first container berths in 1972, before any shipping company had committed to the container trade between Europe and Asia-Pacific, and container traffic grew rapidly, to the point that in 1990, Singapore was handling more containers than any port globally. It is currently the world's top trans-shipment hub, feeding trans-shipments to smaller ports, which lack deep water or cannot afford investing in facilities that would enable container handling.[45] Singapore has also been ranked the world's most important maritime centre in terms of shipping, law and finance, logistics and ports, and competitiveness, putting it on par with other leading cities like London, Oslo, Rotterdam and Shanghai.[46] Can this position be sustained? The ambition is there, but Singapore's chief weakness is a shortage of human capital — will it be able to build a strong core of local talent to maintain its maritime sector?[47]

But what next? An open city-state sustained by global flows will face tensions when it has also to function as a nation state. Even as Singapore has evolved into a modern city-state, and its port functions may be overtaken by other economic roles, does its future growth and development demand that it continues to rely on its development instincts as a port city? The requirements of an international clientele and an open economy on the one hand, and the needs and aspirations of its local citizenry on the other, are not always complementary. More fundamentally, the construction of national identity will be subjected to the shifting strains of the myriad of cultural forms and traditions that are characteristic of a port city.

The tensions and contradictions of a city that is also a country will be the subject of my next lecture.

---

[44] Siddique, *Asian Port Cities, 53.*

[45] Perry, *Singapore: Unlikely Power*, 206–8.

[46] Jakobsen et al., "The Leading Maritime Capitals of the World 2017."

[47] Perry, *Singapore: Unlikely Power*, 261.

Question-and-Answer Session

Moderated by Professor Chua Beng Huat

Professor Chua Beng Huat: I wish to make three observations before we open the floor to questions.

The first point is about our cosmopolitanism. That was a very important observation by Professor Tan Tai Yong about our past. The current multicultural and multiracial composition of our population has its beginnings in our economic activities as an emporium of trade, and that, in turn, influenced public culture. Singapore's cultural orientation, as Prof. Tan said, has always been fairly cosmopolitan, and cosmopolitanism recognises and lives with differences.

As Prof. Tan observed, by the early 20th century, Singapore had become the heart of the intellectual world of Southeast Asia, and a gathering point for Malay intellectual and political thinkers. Many of the radical Malay thinkers also published their material in Singapore.

Furthermore, Singapore was a place of refuge for Chinese intellectuals escaping the civil war in mainland China, who brought their modernist thought to Chinese schools here. Singapore's Indian population was also very much concerned with the independence movement and religious debate that was going on in India. As such, these groups constituted a very vibrant intellectual community in Singapore.

However, with the emergence of the nation, and our population becoming increasingly locally born, Singapore and being Singaporean have become things we can invest in and identify with emotionally. Unfortunately, to a certain extent, nationalism has narrowed our culture and outlook. The external orientation, openness and cosmopolitanism of the past have declined.

My second point is about urban public culture. Prof. Tan has shown that the port continues to be a very significant part of Singapore's economy. The importance of the port extends beyond Singapore's harbour, because PSA International, formerly Port of Singapore Authority, now operates many ports around the world. However, the port's role here has changed over time. In my childhood, the port was a very important part of everyday life, because it was a major employer, directly and indirectly, of a very significant portion of the population. Unfortunately, the culture that flourished because of the port, the so-called "romance of the port", has largely disappeared.

Anson Road used to have bars, sex workers — all kinds of sleaze that came with the port. That was part of the romance. Now, that, along with the accompanying literature and commentary, has disappeared. The centrality of the port, in spite of its economic importance, has disappeared from our everyday life.

My third point is the myth of Singapore's sustainability. For the longest time, we always said, especially in the 1960s, that as an independent island nation, we could not possibly survive economically, which explains why the battle for Merger was so intense. As Prof. Tan said, the stability that arose from Singapore's status as staple port in the 1930s and 1940s led us to forget the fact that we had always been a global node rather than just a part of the Malay peninsula. I think it is important to be reminded, as Prof. Tan nicely put it, of that occasion of historical amnesia. It is also important to recall our vibrancy before the early 20th century, as there is a connection between this and the idea of the global city that was reinvigorated in the 1970s by Rajaratnam.

My discomfort does not lie with the historical trajectory laid out by Prof. Tan, but more with the question of the present. In the past, Singapore had a very liberal immigration policy. That has radically changed now. We are harsh on low-income migrants, forgetting that our own ancestors were largely low-income migrants.

I would like to hear Prof. Tan's thoughts on the topic of intellectual vibrancy and cosmopolitanism. I think our desire, anxiety and need to build a nation, has narrowed our view of ourselves, and made us more conservative in outlook now. London and New York are important comparisons, but we are nowhere close to being as complex in racial composition as London or New York.

Professor Tan Tai Yong: I agree. The idea of Singapore as a nation state is about 50 years old. But Singapore has a much longer history and, in its longer existence, it has evolved in very interesting ways. We are now a nation state with constraints and challenges.

I do not know if the nation state or a more open, liberal cosmopolitan port city will be Singapore's normal state in future. These are questions we need to ask ourselves. While nation states have certain imperatives, technology has made the world more interconnected and open. This has led to disruptions, and the question is how Singapore should respond: Can Singapore return to being a vibrant, cosmopolitan community, or will it be more constrained and nationalistic? I compared Singapore with Hong Kong, London, and New York, but these are global cities with natural hinterlands, unlike Singapore.

Prof. Chua: I will now open the floor for questions.

Participant: You mentioned that, at some point, one quarter of our exports had been tin. I would have thought a lot of the tin would be in north Malaya, and closer to Penang. Why did tin end up being processed and exported out of Singapore, rather than other port cities?

Prof. Tan: Singapore developed as a hub and staple port in several ways. First, Singapore was able to process and export commodities from Malaya very quickly because of its transport infrastructure. It also had a complex system of trade and credit — big British agency houses like Guthrie and Sime Darby had operations here, and there were also local trading houses. Singapore was able to develop into a hub that incorporated and streamlined numerous functions such as refining, export and trade. That is why it was the key staple port for the Malay peninsula.

Singapore was a major coaling station when the steamship came into play and the Suez Canal opened. This is another example of Singapore creating opportunities for itself and keeping up with changes, which has ensured Singapore's evolution, success and survival throughout its history.

Participant: What do you see as threats and opportunities for Singapore going forward? If the East Coast Rail Link in Malaysia goes ahead, will it threaten Singapore's port? Further north, from time to time, we hear about the building of the canal across the Isthmus of Kra. Even further north, with the melting of the polar ice caps, if this provides a shorter route from the Pacific Ocean to the Atlantic Ocean, across the Arctic Ocean, how would that affect Singapore's status as a port city?

Prof. Tan: Singapore will always face challenges, and its competitive advantages can be eroded very quickly.

You could be a maritime trading entrepôt, but what do you do when entrepôt trade declines? With commodities coming out of Malaya, how do you position yourself as a staple port?

Similarly, today, in the current form of port management, Singapore has to stay ahead of the game or risk being overtaken.

I remember, as a student, we were always very proud of the fact that Singapore was the busiest port in the world. Historically, Singapore's location was attractive to the British, who wanted to impose some control over the trade that was flowing through the Straits of Melaka, and compete against the Dutch East Indies. However, this locational advantage may not be permanent, and as I said in my previous lecture, while we may think that our location gives our port an advantage over others, ports in Tanjung Pelepas and Pasir Gudang essentially share the same location. As such, the way forward is not to just sit back and enjoy the strategic advantage of location, but to stay ahead by creating opportunities to do better. I think Hong Kong is experiencing similar challenges in the face of competition from Chinese ports.

If you cut through the Isthmus of Kra, people probably will not need to sail that far south to Singapore. But Singapore can still try to leverage its airports and other forms of technology to stay ahead.

With regard to the melting of the polar ice caps, I was initially tickled when I found out that Singapore was a member of the Arctic Council. I wondered why Singapore wanted to be a member. But I realised, if the polar ice caps melt and a shipping passage is opened there, we had better be in a position to find out how that will affect us, and make decisions about new trade routes that may emerge.

A leader in Singapore once commented that Singapore is always 10 years away from a disaster. He meant that if we were not alert and fail to reinvent ourselves, something will hit us eventually. Anticipating problems decades ahead is critical for the survival of Singapore.

Participant: I was very taken by your comment that Singapore, as a result of its status as a port city, became a hub for intellectual development and foment in the 19th century. I was wondering if you could shed more light on how that has developed up to the present day, and comment on what Singapore's intellectual and cultural footprint could be.

Prof. Tan: For the first part of your question, may I refer you to my last lecture, which you can find on the IPS website, because I spent quite a bit of time discussing how Singapore was the centre of Malay printing and newspapers, how groups came from the surrounding regions, used printing technology, and started different newspapers. I also went into some detail in discussing how Singapore was the centre of Haj activities in the region.

Colonial officials were always worried that radicals, reformists and revolutionaries were congregating in Singapore because of our openness as a port city and a flourishing print culture. They could spread their ideas through publications like newspapers and, given the connections between port cities, ideas would spread to Rangoon, Calcutta and Penang, especially with the onset of submarine telegraphy.

However, in the name of nation building, there had to be some uniformity as Singapore became a country rather unexpectedly in 1965, when it separated from Malaysia. There was a need to build structures of state, define what it meant to be a Singapore citizen, have a vision of what it meant to belong to a country, be a nation state in a community of nations; to think about Singapore nationalism, in place of Malayan nationalism. However, going forward, we may have to rethink our approach, because what served us well in the past may not continue to do so in the future. We may have to be more open and adventurous, and ask more difficult questions in imagining our future.

Participant: You talk about this idea of opening up. What does that mean, and what does it imply?

Prof Tan: It means a number of things. Being open to offering different types of education is one example. Education can be vocational, and provide people with the knowledge to function in the manufacturing economy. Education can also be a means of encouraging people to think out of the box. I am making a pitch for Yale-NUS College, which offers a liberal arts education.

Another aspect is being open to exploring different ideas. People should be able to push boundaries, and think of different possibilities. This constitutes a cultural change, where organic effervescence and a multitude of ideas can co-exist with an effective and forward-looking government.

As citizens of a country, we should not simply depend on the government for all the answers, especially in thinking about the future.

Participant: How do you reconcile the two contrasting narratives that Singapore has — one, that we are always looking out for economic opportunities and focused on economic growth, and two, that there is more that defines Singapore as a nation?

Prof. Tan: I do not see the goal of economic growth and the question of national identity as mutually exclusive. These goals and concerns exist for all national entities.

Participant: Can Singaporeans also identify ourselves as global citizens?

Prof. Tan: I think people are increasingly identifying themselves beyond the nation state. Identities are very complex and multi-layered. All of us have in ourselves different types of identities. For instance, a well-travelled Singaporean may identify with issues of the world and yet remain a loyal, committed citizen of the country. There is no conflict in those multiple identifications.

Prof. Chua: Thank you Prof. Tan, and have a good evening everyone.

Lecture IV

THE IDEA OF SINGAPORE
City, Country and Nation

LECTURE IV

In my last lecture, I referred to Singapore as a port city, both in terms of functions and instincts. At various times in history, Singapore has been described as emporium, trading hub and cosmopolis. How would I describe Singapore today? Most obviously, it is a country. More accurately, it is a sovereign nation state. Invariably, Singapore has been called a city-state, and increasingly, a global city-state.

All this is to suggest that Singapore has, over time, morphed from one form to another, largely determined by historical circumstances. Singaporean author and poet, Alvin Pang put it eloquently when he said:

> *Our story was not inscribed whole upon some tabula rasa: no nation's is. Building upon countless elements old and new, from near and far — whether imposed, inherited, invented or fashioned anew to suit — the Singapore we have today is the outcome of a long continuum of accommodation, adaptation, reimagining and risk. More to the point: we are not done with our changes. We continue to become.*[1]

---

[1] Alvin Pang, "City of a Thousand Histories; Island of a Thousand Cities," in *The Birthday Book: What Should We Never Forget*, eds. Sheila Pakir and Malminderjit Singh (Singapore: Ethos, 2017), 9.

Throughout its history, Singapore has continuously evolved, taking on different forms. At this point, its status as city and country is most salient. It is a nation state that grew out of a city. Major cities in the past have become part of larger nation states: Venice in Italy, Hamburg in Germany, and Penang and Melaka in Malaysia. But Singapore's experience is unique in that the city became the country.

I shall now try to narrate how this came to be and examine how Singapore's evolution was not a straightforward and predictable trajectory. Singapore's history took unexpected turns and its current incarnation as a country and city carries tensions and paradoxes that continue to animate its development and growth.

Post-war political developments

The official narrative has it that the seeds of Singaporean nationalism were sown in the immediate aftermath of World War II, an outcome of the British surrender to the Japanese and the ensuing Occupation. The shock and trauma that followed the calamitous defeat of an imperial power at the hands of an Asian country triggered major political repercussions throughout the European empires in Asia. There was indeed political awakening in Singapore in the aftermath of the Pacific War. But it was not the sort of nascent nationalism that grew into mass-based movements or revolutionary wars of the type seen in India, Indonesia, Burma and Indo-China.

The disruptions caused by the War and its aftermath created the conditions for widespread anti-colonial feelings. The old colonial order was no longer viable and had to be replaced. The main political force that challenged the legitimacy of continued colonialism was the communists. Galvanised by their successes as freedom fighters during the Japanese Occupation, the Malayan Communist Party was the first organised political force to mobilise locals to act against the unjust colonial system. By the late 1940s, the communists were a force to be reckoned with; they took to subverting the colonial state by infiltrating trade unions and student organisations, and by launching highly disruptive strikes and direct political action against the authorities. This was an anti-colonial insurrection and an attempt at sparking a popular revolution. The Communist Party and their sympathisers not only wanted to end colonialism, but desired to replace the old, traditional political and social order with a new, independent, socialist system.

The British responded with a slew of regulations, the most severe of which were the Emergency Regulations, applied to Malaya and Singapore, when a communist-led insurgency erupted in Malaya in 1948. The Communist Party of Malaya was outlawed and its networks curtailed. This drove the communists and left-wing movement underground, but they did not totally dissipate.

While the left-wing movement had local political objectives — the end of colonial rule — its political language was international. Local left-wing activists drew inspiration from liberation movements elsewhere in the Afro-Asian world. Their horizons and expectations were broadened by the end of empire in South Asia, Indonesia and Indo-China, together with Pan-Africanism, Pan-Arabism and the Afro-Asian Conference in Bandung.[2] Much of left-wing politics was shaped by the rise of Chinese communism as an anti-imperialist and nationalistic ideology. The idea of a socialist future that promised a just and equal society, especially for the working classes, appealed to Chinese-educated youths in Singapore and Malaya, who saw the colonial state as exploitative and unjust. This was not solely a local contest for political power, determining who would take over from the departing imperialists. It was a fight to determine what type of state and society would replace the colonial state.

But the British were not about to make it easy for these revolutionaries. Decolonisation had to be managed such that British interests could be maintained in post-colonial Asia. In Malaya and Singapore, the British showed that they were prepared to devolve political power to moderate

---

[2] T.N. Harper, "Lim Chin Siong and the 'Singapore Story'", in *Comet in Our Sky: Lim Chin Siong in History*, eds. Tan Jing Quee and Jomo K. S. (Kuala Lumpur: Insan, 2001), 16–17.

groups, while taking draconian measures to beat down the left-wing radicals. It was a well-worn tactic used by the British in their Asian and African colonies, to search for political successors — nationalists though they may be — who would be prepared to continue doing business with the British after the end of empire. The French and Dutch took a different approach, and the outcomes in their colonies were significantly different from those of the British colonies in Southeast Asia.

When the British instituted political reforms to take the sting out of anti-colonial attacks, political parties surfaced in Singapore to contest elections. By the mid-1950s, the political climate had changed. The introduction of mass-based electoral politics would set the stage for a political contest to decide who would eventually bring an end to colonial rule and determine the future of Singapore. With tough security instruments and legislation to curtail left-wing activism, the way was paved for a peaceful transfer of power to a popularly elected government that took over a self-governing Singapore in 1959. While initially distrustful of the People's Action Party (PAP), the British eventually came around, and saw them as the most viable party to which political power could be transferred. The British were keen to preserve Singapore as a port city and naval base, and planned to re-integrate it with Malaya in due course. By the late 1950s, London had concocted a plan known as the "Grand Design", which aimed at ultimately bringing together all its Southeast Asian colonies into a super-federation anchored on peninsular Malaya. Singapore, which had already been given city status in 1951, elevating it from a town to a city,[3] would be a key piece in the "Grand Design". The next step was self-government and integration with Malaya.[4]

The gradual devolution of power from the British to local politicians was, therefore, not predicated on the expression of some form of

---

[3] National Library Board Singapore, "Singapore is Conferred City Status — Singapore History, 22nd Sep 1951," HistorySG, 2014, http://eresources.nlb.gov.sg/history/events/7333873b-d517-4a75-b828-331a30673b30#1.

[4] Tan Tai Yong, *Creating "Greater Malaysia": Decolonization and the Politics of Merger* (Singapore: Institute of Southeast Asian Studies, 2008), 13–28.

Singaporean nationalism. While anti-colonial politics did become a potent force, the British were able to dictate the pace and form of decolonisation in Singapore. As Singapore prepared for self-government in the late 1950s, the expectation was that the next step in its political evolution would be independence from colonial rule by joining Malaya as part of a larger Federation.

Malayan nationalism

The desire to end colonial rule did not necessarily translate into the political ambition to achieve independence for Singapore. While Singapore had to be politically separated from the Malay peninsula in 1946 as an expedient to "retain a base for British activity in Southeast Asia",[5] no one in Singapore believed that the island state would eventually strike out on its own. The exclusion of Singapore from the Malayan Union scheme, and subsequently the Federation, was seen as temporary; the British as well as local politicians of all stripes believed that Singapore had to eventually return to Malaya.

The PAP's ultimate objective was to achieve independence for Singapore through Merger. This was borne out of a conviction that Singapore had no economic future if it were not re-integrated with the Malayan hinterland. From a political and security standpoint, Singapore would be too vulnerable on its own, and would succumb to radical left-wing takeover unless it was fortified by the bulwark of the right-wing Malayan state.

So Lee Kuan Yew and the PAP campaigned not for an independent nation state of Singapore in the late 1950s and early 1960s, but for merger with Malaya. Lee had argued that "merger was inevitable" and prepared the city-state to join the Malayan state. From 1959, Lee took steps to encourage a pan-Malayan outlook in Singapore with the hope of creating, in his own words, a "Malayanised Singapore man who could talk, think

---

[5]   Nicholas Tarling, "Part Two: Problems and Policies — Nationalism," in *Nations and States in Southeast Asia* (Cambridge: Cambridge University Press, 1998), 77.

and act like the exemplary Malayans of the Federation."[6] To facilitate the social integration of Singapore's predominantly Chinese population into the Malayan hinterland, Malay was made Singapore's national language and a Malay Head of State (or Yang di-Pertuan Negara) was installed. A Malay Education Advisory Committee was set up in 1959, and a Malayan school syllabus introduced.

Singapore became a state in Malaysia in September 1963. It did so on special terms. As a state of the Federation, Singapore would enjoy a much higher level of autonomy than all the other states in Malaysia, but the trade-off was that Singapore would also have lower representation in the federal parliament, and was not expected to partake in the politics of the peninsula. The Tunku had envisioned that Singapore could continue to prosper economically as a port city, with Malaya as its hinterland. However, political control of the Federation would have to remain in Kuala Lumpur. In the Tunku's mind, Singapore could be the New York of the Federation, while Kuala Lumpur would be the Washington DC.[7]

Independence

In August 1965, very unexpectedly, Singapore became an independent sovereign state. The Merger project had failed and Singapore was excised, once again, from its Malayan hinterland. This time, there could be no return to the British empire as a Crown Colony. Nor was there another Federation to which Singapore could append itself. An exit from the state of Malaysia meant that Singapore had to stand on its own as a sovereign state, occupying its place in a post-war world order that was organised as a collection of nation states.

Singapore did not plan to be a sovereign state, but it had sovereignty thrust upon it. What were the chances of small, sovereign states surviving? The historian Arnold Toynbee, writing in 1966, had opined that as a sovereign

---

[6] Mohamed Noordin Sopiee, *From Malayan Union to Singapore Separation: Political Unification in the Malaysia Region, 1945–65* (Kuala Lumpur: Penerbit Universiti Malaya, 1974), 116.

[7] Tan Tai Yong, *Creating "Greater Malaysia"*, 124.

independent city-state, Singapore was "too small a political unit to be practicable."[8] Lee Kuan Yew, too, once said, "In the context of the second half of the 20th century South-East Asia, island nations are political jokes."[9]

While the nation state might appear to be a very natural political organisation today, it is, unlike the city, a relatively new phenomenon in history. Nation states in Europe mainly emerged in the 19th century, in the wake of the French Revolution. They proliferated in the 20th century, following World War I. In 1920, the League of Nations had about 50 members. The 1815 Treaty of Vienna, which represented the international community then, had only eight signatories, of which three were empires (Austria-Hungary, Russia and Turkey). After World War II, as empires broke up and erstwhile colonies had to be re-constituted as nation states, their numbers grew. The United Nations now has nearly 200 members. As new nation states emerged, many continued to struggle with the tasks of delineating boundaries and uniting disparate communities and geographical entities. Benedict Anderson calls the nation state an "imagined community", and even today, nation states are seen as younger enterprises (in the long history of political organisations) that have yet to prove their viability.[10] Cities have been around for over 5,000 years, while most nation states are barely a century old.

Building state and nation

In all its earlier incarnations, Singapore had functioned as a city of sorts. It was an emporium, a cosmopolis, a colonial port city, a crown colony and then a city within a larger Malaysian Federation. But it was a most unnatural nation. It did not have any of the ingredients needed to build national identity — indigenous rootedness, civilisational lineage, or cultural, religious, ethnic and linguistic homogeneity; all it had was perhaps a common political cause.

[8] Arnold Toynbee, cited in John Curtis Perry, Singapore: *Unlikely Power* (New York: Oxford University Press, 2017), 177.

[9] Constitutional Talks in London, *Singapore Legislative Assembly Debates,* 1st ser., vol. 3 (5 March 1957), col. 1457.

[10] Ricky Burdett and Deyan Sudjic, *The Endless City* (London: Phaidon Press, 2007), cited in Simon Curtis, "Introduction," in *Global Cities and Global Order* (Oxford and New York: Oxford University Press, 2016), 6.

The politics in the island up to 1965 had reflected its historical experience as an open port city and the international make-up of the cosmopolis. Internationalism and populism, more than the indigenous nationalism that emerged in India, for example, was the natural experience in Singapore from the 1920s to the 1950s. Thus, the idea of Singapore as a nation state sat uncomfortably with its instincts as an open commercial cosmopolis. Yet, in 1965 Singapore had become a nation state, very much against its leaders' expectations. It now had to get on with the business of quickly reconstituting and re-imagining itself. It knew how to be a city, but becoming a nation state, with hardly any time to prepare, was a different proposition altogether.

Two processes had to happen simultaneously, each reinforcing the other. The first was state building, and alongside it, nation building. The process of state-building after 1965 was driven by a single-minded devotion to the goal of survival. Building on the structural foundations of the colonial state, Singapore focused on getting its economy right, establishing functioning governing institutions, educating and housing its people and creating an efficient bureaucracy to develop and implement policies. Singapore became a viable state with a thriving economy and efficient system of governance with the wherewithal to feed, house and educate its citizens. To defend its national territory and sovereignty, Singapore had to build its defence capabilities and the Singapore Armed Forces came into being. Next, a diplomatic service was developed for the state to conduct relations with other states.

This fed into the process of nation building, which needed a much longer time. It has been argued that "nationalism [or national identity] … is not a phenomenon that appears suddenly. It is a result of a process by which a people become conscious of themselves as a separate national entity in the modern world, a process by which they become willing to transfer their primary loyalty from the village, or the region, or the monarch, to the nation state."[11]

---

[11] William J. Duiker, *The Rise of Nationalism in Vietnam: 1900–1941* (Ithaca and London: Cornell University Press, 1976), 15.

As a new nation state, Singapore had to instil in its people a sense of community, and emphasise its viability — no matter how small it was — in a world of nation states. But, in the case of Singapore, this consciousness could not be built on the foundations of a common culture. Neither did the country have a long, shared history, or common struggle, on which to meld common purpose. As former minister George Yeo said, "Singapore nationalism had to be cooked in a hurry without the fire of war or revolution."[12]

Nation building — the building of an intrinsic national identity — was therefore a much more complicated enterprise than state building. How do you generate a lasting sense of identity, bonding and loyalty among a diverse and largely migrant population, whose identification with the state dated back only a few years before 1965, when citizenship was introduced in 1957? The population, until August 1965, had been told that they were Malaysian citizens, and now had to embrace a different identity as citizens of a new country. This was a wholly new experience for the people of Singapore, most of whom had never thought that Singapore could be independent, let alone a nation.

Lee Kuan Yew made this very clear when he said:

We ask ourselves, what is a Singaporean? In the first place we did not want to be Singaporeans. We wanted to be Malayans. Then the idea was extended and we decided to be Malaysians. But, twenty-three months of Malaysia — a traumatic experience for all parties in Malaysia — ended rather abruptly with our being Singaporeans.[13]

---

[12] George Yeo, *George Yeo on Bonsai, Banyan and the Tao*, eds. Asad-ul Iqbal Latif and Lee Huay Leng (Singapore: World Scientific, 2015), 49.

[13] Lee Kuan Yew, cited in Michael Hill and Lian Kwen Fee, *The Politics of Nation Building and Citizenship in Singapore* (London: Routledge, 1995), 12; Lee Kuan Yew, "Transcript of Speech by the Prime Minister, Mr Lee Kuan Yew, at the Reunion Dinner of St. Andrew's Old Boys' Association on 7th September, 1968," September 7, 1968, http://www.nas.gov.sg/archivesonline/data/pdfdoc/lky19680907.pdf.

From 1965, political leaders urged the people of Singapore to think of themselves as Singaporeans, not as Chinese, Malays, Indians and Sri Lankans. But up to this point, Singapore had no experience of being a nation and people were not accustomed to being Singaporean.[14]

Survivalism

Lee Kuan Yew declared in December 1965 that "independence ... create[d] the conditions for the eventual success of what we want: survival in Southeast Asia ... as a separate and distinct people." He described Southeast Asia as "a very turbulent part of the world" and warned that Singapore had to be careful not to be "absorbed or swallowed up by ... bigger hordes."[15]

And so the narrative of survivalism became a creed that was used to bind people together. But it was not just the fear of perishing that was used to build common purpose. The state would use a combination of economic and social development, in the context of political stability, to build belief in the new nation state. Development and growth would be undergirded by shared values and beliefs that promised every citizen a chance to progress and prosper in a country of their own, regardless of race, religion and socioeconomic status. Thus, the centrality of the principles of meritocracy and multiculturalism in Singapore.

Diversity had to be managed in the name of nationalism. Emphasising Singapore's multiculturalism was important because the 1964 race riots were still fresh in the memories of the government and its people. In many ways, the conception of the Singaporean nation grew out of its bitter experiences in Malaysia. As David Chang writes, after Singapore's separation from Malaysia, "'Malaysian Malaysia' ... found its experimentation in [Lee Kuan Yew's] own multiracial, multi-lingual and multi-religious nation."[16]

---

[14] S Rajaratnam, quoted in Perry, *Singapore: Unlikely Power*, 117.

[15] Lee Kuan Yew, "Transcript of a Speech in English by the Prime Minister at a Luncheon Given by the Pasir Panjang Residents at Perak House on 5th December, 1965," December 5, 1965, http://www.nas.gov.sg/archivesonline/data/pdfdoc/lky19651205b.pdf.

[16] David W. Chang, "Nation-Building in Singapore," *Asian Survey* 8, no. 9 (1968): 766.

The PAP government adopted policies that actively managed Singapore's ethnic diversity. For instance, in the early post-independence years, PAP leaders tried to downplay the "Chinese-ness" of Singapore to avoid being perceived as a "Third China" by its neighbours. The special position of the Malays was also recognised in Singapore's Constitution, with the designation of Malay as the national language, and the recognition of the special position of the Malays, committing the government to "promote their political, educational, religious, economic, social and cultural interests."[17] At the same time, four official languages were selected — English, Malay, Mandarin and Tamil — to be used in official documents, parliament, and schools.[18] In the early years of independence, projecting the image of Singapore as both a harmonious patchwork of cultures and an English-speaking nation took precedence over highlighting cultural distinctions and heritage.

The flag, national anthem and pledge were important symbols of ideals and aspirations that would bind Singaporeans as a people, building the nation as a "community of destiny". But loyalty and identity had to be nurtured and anchored on concrete experiences. National Service and the educational system became key vehicles for creating and sustaining national identity, and a successful public housing scheme, as well as a growing economy, provided stability and belief in the nation.

This is not to say that all nation-building efforts have been unambiguously positive. Some scholars view Singapore's policy of multiculturalism as "an instrument of social control and policing of boundaries in the name of the larger public good and harmony."[19] Another critique of the policy is that it functions as a tool for disempowerment. By encouraging strong racial

---

[17] Attorney-General's Chambers, "Constitution of the Republic of Singapore Part XIII — General Provisions — Article 152: Minorities and Special Position of Malays," Singapore Statutes Online, accessed 17 June 2019, https://sso.agc.gov.sg/Act/CONS1963?ValidDate=20170401&ProvIds=P1XIII-.

[18] Jon S. T. Quah, "Globalization and Singapore's Search for Nationhood," in *Nationalism and Globalization: East and West*, ed. Leo Suryadinata (Singapore: Institute of Southeast Asian Studies, 2000), 81–82.

[19] Raka Shome, "Mapping the Limits of Multiculturalism in the Context of Globalization," *International Journal of Communication* 6 (2012): 160.

group identification, state multiracialism theoretically prevents claims of cultural otherness or cultural discrimination.[20] It has been argued that multiculturalism pushes race out of the front line of politics, while still according it high visibility in the cultural sphere.[21] As such, this ideology that had served Singapore well in its search for national identity early on may have to be tweaked moving forward.

Return to the cosmopolis?

After decades of state and nation building, Singapore has established itself as a viable nation state. It now has all the characteristics of a nation state — territory, sovereignty, citizens, and a legitimate government. But the inherent dilemmas of a new nation state that grew out of an old commercial city that privileged openness, mobility and connectivity have not gone away. Intense global competition has awakened the instincts of the cosmopolis, notwithstanding the demands of nurturing a local base of citizens. Historian Anthony Reid points out that "[by the end of the 20th century] ... as increasing global competition created an international context where [the cosmopolis] was more necessary than ever ... the public rhetoric of nation appeared both less necessary in itself and less opposed to cosmopolis. Public leaders appealed to make Singapore ... 'a cosmopolitan centre, able to attract, retain and absorb talent from all over the world,'[22] or 'a global hub where people, ideas and capital come together.'"[23] This has generated the tensions that are innate to a country that is a city.

---

[20] Ibid.

[21] Chua Beng Huat, "Racial Singaporeans: Absence after the Hyphen," in *Southeast Asian Identities: Culture and the Politics of Representation in Indonesia, Malaysia, Singapore, and Thailand*, ed. Joel S. Kahn (Singapore: Institute of Southeast Asian Studies, 1998), 28–50.

[22] Lee Kuan Yew, "How Will Singapore Compete in a Global Economy (Speech by Senior Minister Lee Kuan Yew to Nanyang Technological University (NTU)/National University of Singapore (NUS) Students, Tue 15 Feb 2000)," Ministry of Information and the Arts and The Arts, February 15, 2000, http://www.nas.gov.sg/archivesonline/speeches/view-html?filename=2000021502.htm, quoted in Anthony Reid, "Cosmopolis and Nation in Central Southeast Asia," Asia Research Institute Working Paper Series, 22 (April 2004): 11.

[23] Goh Chok Tong, 1999, speech at opening of parliament, quoted in Reid, "Cosmopolis and Nation," 11.

Director of the Institute of Policy Studies Janadas Devan has argued, "The fact that this city is all the country that we will have informs every facet of our existence." As such, Singapore the city and country needs to be an "exceptionally and intricately well-organised organism", or risk not existing at all.[24] He referred to Singapore's key infrastructure to illustrate how Singapore being a country means it has to, among other things, house its gateways (port and airport), manufacturing and military facilities within its geographical limits. Given that public infrastructure and housing occupy well over half of Singapore's land area, it is inevitable that some decisions will give importance to certain goals while sacrificing others. For the authorities, managing Singapore as a city and country with small land area, amidst other challenges, has necessitated intense, long-term planning, and prominent government presence.

Let me cite two examples where the Singapore government has had to mediate the contradictory pulls of "internationalisation/regionalisation vs Singapore as home" and that of "attracting foreign talent vs looking after Singaporeans."[25]

Example one: Immigration

Decisions on arguably pragmatic and expedient grounds have not necessarily continued to produce positive results. One example is Singapore's liberal immigration policies, which at its peak, ran the risk of alienating the local population and contributed to xenophobic sentiments. Liberal immigration policies were and are part of the government's plan to develop Singapore into a "talent capital", attract migrants to fill the gap in manpower needs given Singapore's greying population, and ultimately sustain its economic growth.

---

[24] Janadas Devan, "Exceptional Government to Sustain a Nation Once Thought Improbable," January 23, 2017, https://www.ipscommons.sg/exceptional-government-to-sustain-a-nation-once-thought-improbable/.

[25] Brenda S. A. Yeoh and T. C. Chang, "Globalising Singapore: Debating Transnational Flows in the City," *Urban Studies* 38, no. 7 (2001): 1028.

However, the non-resident population increased at an unprecedented pace in the first decade of the 21st century, resulting in widespread public disapproval of the government's liberal immigration policies for highly skilled labour around the 2011 general elections.[26] Another wave of anti-immigrant sentiment among the local population, which arose when the Population White Paper was released in 2013, illustrated the continued tensions between the needs of the city-state and the sentiments of the nation state's citizens. Since then, the government has continued to reassure Singaporeans that the workforce is not disproportionately dependent on foreign labour. Its stance is that foreign talent complements rather than competes with the local workforce, even as it plans to reduce the number of employment passes it grants to qualified foreigners.[27]

With hindsight, some would argue that too quick an inflow of foreign workers depressed wages among low-wage workers.[28] The impact of a large inflow, if not adequately mitigated, would put pressure on any country's infrastructure and stresses on the local population, among other social costs. While workers from abroad filled gaps in roles in sectors such as construction, health and social services, some locals have perceived foreigners to be taking from Singapore's economic pie rather than growing it. Further, there continues to be resentment towards skilled workers who had been granted Permanent Residency, who are viewed as enjoying the benefits of citizenship without having to take on the attendant obligations.[29] As for "low-skilled" workers, they are "forgotten" even as they have grown

---

[26] Brenda Yeoh and Weiqiang Lin, "Rapid Growth in Singapore's Immigrant Population Brings Policy Challenges," Migration Policy Institute, April 3, 2012, https://www.migrationpolicy.org/article/rapid-growth-singapores-immigrant-population-brings-policy-challenges.

[27] Government of Singapore, "Do You Know How Many Types of Foreign Workers We Have in Singapore?" Factually (Ministry of Communications and Information website), March 2013, http://www.gov.sg/factually/content/do-you-know-how-many-types-of-foreign-workers-we-have-in-singapore; Angela Teng, "The Big Read: The Foreigner Issue — Are We Ready for a Rethink?" *TODAYonline*, February 3, 2018, https://www.todayonline.com/singapore/big-read-foreigner-issue-are-we-ready-rethink.

[28] Manu Bhaskaran, "An Architect of the Singapore Miracle," *The Business Times*, March 25, 2015, https://www.businesstimes.com.sg/government-economy/lee-kuan-yew-dies/an-architect-of-the-singapore-miracle.

[29] Yeoh and Chang, "Globalising Singapore," 1031.

increasingly visible as part of Singapore's social landscape and public spaces. Singapore aspires to be a cosmopolis, but the cosmopolitanism in Singapore has its clear limits.

At the same time, these attitudes are not cast in stone. The Institute of Policy Studies' 2016 survey on the emigration attitudes of young Singaporeans found that more respondents thought that Singapore benefitted from the presence of "foreign talent", compared to respondents in 2010. At the same time, there were also more respondents (2016 versus 2010) who thought that having too much foreign talent could dilute the cohesiveness of society.[30]

Example two: Developing the arts

Another example was the pushback from the ground in response to state efforts to develop Singapore as a prominent arts destination and hub. Government efforts to quickly and visibly shape Singapore into a global city for the arts were not well received by local arts practitioners. A former Artistic Director of The Substation argued that the hub model would "retard the growth of our indigenous arts development" because it prioritised massive infrastructural development, import of foreign specialists, and tourism, over benefits to local practitioners and smaller-scale development projects. Some criticised the government's motives — nurturing arts and culture as a vehicle for economic growth, rather than for their own intrinsic value. Cynics also questioned if "a vibrant arts scene could ever be the result of government blue-prints" and whether an artistic society could be fostered through an economics-driven programme of change.[31]

At the same time, from the government's point of view, attracting international players and supporting local players may be complementary rather than contradictory goals. However, government action has an

---

[30] Gillian Koh, Debbie Soon, and Leong Chan-Hoong, "IPS Survey on Emigration Attitudes of Young Singaporeans (2016)," Institute of Policy Studies, September 28, 2018, https://lkyspp.nus.edu.sg/ips/news/details/ips-survey-on-emigration-attitudes-of-young-singaporeans-2016?fbrefresh=636957795396131050.

[31] Yeoh and Chang, "Globalising Singapore," 1037–8.

outsized footprint and influence in Singapore, compared to other cities, because of our relative smallness and one-city proposition. As such, the tensions between different players that are sometimes natural for cities play out on a national level and become magnified in Singapore's context.

Strengths of a city

But this duality does have its upsides. Singapore has played to its strengths as a city-state, without compromising national identity. As Minister for Finance Heng Swee Keat said in his 2019 Budget speech, "As a city-state, we are nimbler and can adapt to changes faster." Singapore can also take advantage of its strategic location and "serve as a neutral, trusted node in key spheres of global activities."[32]

Former minister George Yeo also expounded on the advantages a city-state possesses in regulating its population and resolving urban issues:

> Because we are a city-state and not one city in a large nation state, we are able to solve urban problems which many cities in the world are not able to. A city-state has its own borders. This is its great advantage. It is able to control and regulate the inflow of people. Because of this, Singapore has been able to clear its old slums and prevent new slums from forming. We have better control over our own environment. This is the key reason why we have been able to overcome problems of traffic, pollution, prostitution, drugs, crime, education, housing, health care and so on.... This is one major advantage we have as a city-state.[33]

Positioning itself as a global city offers other advantages. As large nation states turn inwards and intense nationalism generates insularity

---

[32] Heng Swee Keat, "2019 Budget Statement," Ministry of Finance Singapore, February 18, 2019, https://www.singaporebudget.gov.sg/budget_2019/budget-speech.

[33] George Yeo, "Overcoming the Vulnerabilities of a Small Nation (Speech at the Temasek Seminar on 7 November '96)," Ministry of Information and The Arts, November 7, 1996, http://www.nas.gov.sg/archivesonline/speeches/view-html?filename=1996110607.htm.

and protectionism, globally oriented cities could become important international actors in place of nation states. Observers have suggested "this may create new patterns of competition and cooperation in the world, resembling Western Europe when the maritime city-state notably flourished."[34]

Diversity, once regarded as an obstacle to common identity that had to be managed, is now seen as a strength. As contemporary Singapore continues to search for new ways to remain relevant in the global marketplace, it has to welcome people from all around the world in search of investment, work and a better life. This means being open to new immigrants, and seeking ways to integrate these newcomers.

However, as seen from the backlash in response to liberal immigration policies, managing diversity has proven to be a complex task. It is not merely about locals who feel pitted against foreigners, but also about how the state manages different segments and groups within the country that include on the one end "high-waged, highly skilled professional, managerial and entrepreneurial elites," and at the other "low-waged immigrants who occupy insecure niches in the unskilled or semi-skilled sectors of the urban service economy."[35] These groups are affected by globalisation unevenly. Caught in between the two groups are middle-class Singaporeans. Singaporeans generally accept that globalisation has brought economic success to Singapore, but globalisation processes have also brought about change and disruption, such as rising inequality and, for some, a sense of precariousness regarding their livelihoods.[36] As the city's population continues to grow more diverse, its identity also becomes more fluid. One thing is certain: as the canvas grows more colourful, the difficulty lies in blending the colours seamlessly, while ultimately creating a harmonious whole.

---

[34] Perry, *Singapore: Unlikely Power*, 262.

[35] Yeoh and Chang, "Globalising Singapore," 1026.

[36] Anju Mary Paul, *Local Encounters in a Global City: Singapore Stories* (Singapore: Ethos Books, 2017), 16–18.

Local identity and global city: Different sides of the same coin?

The examples of immigration and arts policies show how there are competing needs and wants, which require thoughtful responses and subsequent fine-tuning to ensure Singapore's continued flourishing. Another way of examining these competing goals is to look at them as two differing orientations. There is a part of Singapore that is more oriented towards itself, more inward focused, perhaps closed, even as Singapore also regards itself as outward looking, cosmopolitan, open. As Janadas Devan puts it,

> *I can describe the political, economic and social contradiction between these two Singapores briefly thus: If this island-nation does not remain one of the world's leading global cities, it cannot survive as an economy; we might as well not have left Malaysia. To sustain itself as a leading global city, Singapore must remain open to the world, welcome all varieties of talents, become and remain a cosmopolitan society and culture.*
>
> *To remain a nation, however, Singapore cannot be forever turned determinedly outwards. It cannot be so porous to the outside as to allow itself to be overwhelmed by the foreign. And it cannot resign itself to a diffuse and rootless cosmopolitanism. Life exists here and now, in a particular place and time, or it cannot exist at all.[37]*

Can the division be such a neat one — with Singapore's population being bifurcated into two groups, one internally oriented and the other always looking outwards? Perhaps it is not quite accurate to characterise Singapore as comprising "cosmopolitans" and "heartlanders" that then Prime Minister Goh Chok Tong referred to in his 1999 National Day Rally speech, even if this set of terms provides a starting point for us to think about the internal and external pulls that Singapore negotiates.

---

[37] Janadas Devan, "Opening Remarks at Institute of Policy Studies Annual Flagship Conference Singapore Perspectives 2018," January 22, 2018, https://lkyspp.nus.edu.sg/docs/default-source/ips/singapore-perspectives-2018_opening-remarks_final799d057b46bc6210a3aaff0100138661.pdf.

For then Prime Minister Goh, "cosmopolitans" were defined as English-speaking, international in outlook, and skilled in fields like banking, IT, engineering, science and technology, while "heartlanders" were defined as speaking "Singlish", being local in interest and orientation, making their living within the country, and playing a major role in maintaining core values and social stability.

However, instead of dualistic categories, there is perhaps increasingly a blending of perspectives. Today, more Singaporeans would be more accurately described as "cosmolanders", who "could lead, or could afford to lead, global lifestyles, but prefer the values of the heartlands."[38] This is a form of "rooted cosmopolitanism" that prominent ethicist Kwame Anthony Appiah argues for. The term "rooted cosmopolitanism" seems oxymoronic, for to have roots suggests the need to be embedded in a specific history, nation or people, while to be a cosmopolitan is to declare oneself a citizen of the world. For Appiah, however, these two are inseparable. Local histories, he reminds us, have themselves been shaped by the movements of peoples and their communal practices as old as human history itself. He argues for multiple affiliations, and the idea that one can pledge allegiance to one's country and still conceive of oneself in terms of global identities or universal values.[39]

But, whatever it is, Singapore the nation state cannot close itself off from global capital or labour flows. Its continued desire to be on the winning side of globalisation while maintaining its viability as a nation state means that the government will have to constantly tread a fine line between protectionism and openness. And even as globalisation continues to have a major effect on the culture and cityscape of Singapore, there is the need to navigate it without alienating and leaving behind different groups of people. These could be locals and foreigners who call Singapore home, or Singaporeans who have heeded the call to seek opportunities beyond its shores, but find it difficult

---

[38] Brenda S. A. Yeoh, "Cosmopolitanism and Its Exclusions in Singapore," in *Globalisation and the Politics of Forgetting*, eds. Yong-Sook Lee and Brenda S. A. Yeoh (London: Routledge, 2006), 140–41.

[39] Kwame Anthony Appiah, cited in Jonathan Freedman, "'The Ethics of Identity': A Rooted Cosmopolitan," *The New York Times*, June 12, 2005, https://www.nytimes.com/2005/06/12/books/review/the-ethics-of-identity-a-rooted-cosmopolitan.html.

to maintain ties and relationships with Singapore. Singapore's government has, with time, come to recognise that to attract international companies and human capital, Singapore has to emphasise both our cosmopolitanism and Singapore's "localness". As George Yeo writes, "The tension between being nationalistic and being cosmopolitan cannot be wished away. It has to be gingerly managed." Dogmatic and xenophobic nationalism will "stifle initiative, inhibit trade, and drive [talents] away. It has to be broad minded, practical, idealistic … but also distinctively Singaporean."[40]

Conclusion

In this lecture, I have shown how Singapore has evolved from city to country. For the better part of its existence, it has functioned as an open city, sustained by fluidity, mobility and openness. Its culture was essentially hybrid and cosmopolitan. I argued that, unlike many former Asian colonies, Singapore did not set out to be a nation state once it was freed from colonial rule. Instead, it aspired to be part of something larger by reuniting with the Malayan hinterland. When the Malaysian dream died with Separation, Singapore became an independent nation state and had to strike out on its own. The new state had to work hard to ensure its viability as a new sovereign entity, its size and diversity notwithstanding. In the last half century, it has established itself as a young nation state, but continues to grapple with the fact that it is a city and country in one. These dilemmas will persist as long as there is the desire to "ride the crest of globalisation … while continuing to shape the local arena."[41]

But, I am hopeful. In the title of this lecture, I used the phrase — "The Idea of Singapore". For me, the idea of Singapore refers to the meaning and significance of Singapore; it must be larger than the island itself, and extend beyond its relatively brief existence as a nation state. This may best be encapsulated in the concept of "smallness unconstrained". Smallness may be a central theme in Singapore's history, but it has never constrained the evolution of Singapore as a city, country and nation state.

---

[40] Yeo, *George Yeo on the Bonsai, Banyan and the Tao*, 50.

[41] Yeoh and Chang, "Globalising Singapore," 1028.

Question-and-Answer Session
Moderated by Ms Lydia Lim

Ms Lydia Lim: Professor Tan, you ended on a bright note by saying that, for you, the idea of Singapore is summed up in the phrase, "smallness unconstrained". Going forward, will our smallness continue to be unconstrained? Perhaps the answer lies in something you said at the start of your lecture, that our trajectory could not have been predicted, that it was the result of accommodation, re-imagination and risk-taking, among other things.

The second point I want to pick up on would be the tensions inherent in Singapore being both a global city and a nation, and the challenge of navigating globalisation without alienating or leaving behind different groups of people who call Singapore home. How well is Singapore navigating globalisation while taking care of those who call this place home?

Professor Tan Tai Yong: Balancing these two requires constant calibration. In Singapore's first two decades of nationhood, the priorities were nation and state building. Singapore had to gain the respect of its neighbours and the world. But, in more recent times, Singapore's instincts as a global city have had to come to the fore, as it now has to engage a globalised world. Herein lies the tension, which has to be gingerly managed.

There will always be new challenges, be it labour, immigration, development of the arts, education, or jobs, that Singapore, a city and a country, will have to deal with. Singapore and its government will have to continually negotiate the opposing inclinations of openness and protectionism.

Take me, for example. I work in Yale-NUS College, which is a combination of the global and local. It is a partnership between Yale University, one of the top universities in the United States, and National University of Singapore (NUS), one of the top universities in Asia. The NUS in Yale-NUS' name marks its "localness", but arguably also adds to its international appeal. Yale would not have partnered NUS if not for its reputation and its location in Singapore. There has to be a certain openness in the way the school is run, such as classes, international programmes and on-campus activities because, as a small liberal arts college, Yale-NUS' ethos is different from those of the other universities in Singapore. There is constant negotiation for the space to develop Yale-NUS' distinctiveness as an Asian, and in particular, Singaporean, institution, and also space for international exposure that would benefit not just Singaporeans, but students and faculty from all over the world.

Ms. Lim: Thank you. I think there's a question from a gentleman in the audience.

Participant: Was Singapore expelled from Malaysia, or was Singapore formed as a result of much planning and negotiation? I am of the view that Singapore leaders like Dr Goh Keng Swee and Mr Lee Kuan Yew were consciously planning for the separation. In July 1965, Lee asked E. W. Barker to draft a proclamation of independence, not a proclamation of a looser Federation. So, despite what has been said, their actions show that there was a conscious plan to initiate Separation.

Prof. Tan: Let me first say that the desire for Merger was real. The People's Action Party (PAP) believed fervently that Singapore had no future unless it was part of a larger Federation. There was a period of tough and complex negotiations leading up to the eventual Merger in September 1963 because the Tunku was initially not keen to have Singapore in the Federation. He felt that bringing in an additional one million Chinese would upset the racial arithmetic in Malaysia. He also believed that the Chinese in Singapore were all radicalised or communist sympathisers. He had just faced 12 years of the Malayan Emergency, and the last thing he needed was to further unsettle the politics of the Federation. He remained sceptical throughout the negotiation process.

The Tunku was eventually persuaded by the argument that Singapore was likely to fall to the communists and he would then have the problem of a "Cuba in his Malayan backyard", if Singapore was left out of the Federation. He was advised that it would be easier to deal with the problem if Singapore was one of the states of Malaysia. There were also tough negotiations on various fronts, such as issues of citizenship, sharing of taxes, and Singapore's representation in the Malaysian Parliament. Within a year of Merger, all sorts of problems started to surface.

There were indeed some members of the Singapore Cabinet who believed from very early on, when problems started to surface, that Singapore should try to find a way out of the Federation. Dr Goh Keng Swee was one of them. He was a hard-nosed economist, for whom the common market was a key justification for Merger. But in practice, there was no common market. This was compounded by the fact that the PAP was constantly attacked by the United Malays National Organisation (UMNO) "ultras", who were suspicious of Lee Kuan Yew's political ambitions.

Lee Kuan Yew, in my view, was very conflicted. On the one hand, he really believed in Merger, and on the other, he was faced with numerous problems that seemed intractable. As such, he agreed to let Goh Keng Swee negotiate with Tunku's deputy, Abdul Razak Hussein, on alternative arrangements. Various options were discussed — a looser Federation, Confederation, in the end, all these did not work.

You are right that independence was not a complete shock, or that it was totally unexpected. But this does not mean that Singapore's political leaders planned to exit from the start. They looked for numerous options to try and save the Federation, and ultimately, there was no choice but to leave.

Participant: Could you share your thoughts on early nation building policies and educational policies, such as the Special Assistance Plan (SAP), and how they have made Singapore what it is today?

Prof. Tan: Context is key to understanding our history. In 1965, when Singapore was newly independent, the state needed manpower to develop its industries. As a result, educational policies at the time were geared towards practical functions. Technical skills were prioritised. Lee Kuan Yew famously said that literature was a luxury we could not afford at that time. Then, as Singapore evolved and rose up the value chain, it needed to have the capacity to carry out research and development as its economy and industries became more sophisticated. Education had to develop accordingly.

In my opinion, policies like streaming were implemented to make optimal use of limited resources. However, they had unintended consequences, such as stereotyping, discrimination and inequality. The government recently announced that it would do away with streaming by 2024. Policy has to be responsive, and I think the government has demonstrated their ability to adapt to the times.

As for the SAP, it was started with good intentions. The government wanted to provide avenues for Chinese language and culture to flourish in Singapore. There were also practical reasons, such as the rise of China. However, SAP schools have become tied to the hierarchy of schools in Singapore in terms of perceived quality. Students choose SAP schools mainly because they are thought of as good schools.

Has the SAP programme achieved its purpose? It depends on whom you ask. Some of my students who are products of SAP schools tell me that they have not grown to like the Chinese language despite being products of the SAP system. Others tell me that they have benefited immensely from SAP schools because of the exposure to Chinese culture, literature, and language. Despite the mixed outcomes, I think SAP schools still fulfil a purpose. The question is whether there can be more diversity in SAP schools. If these schools produce students who only know fellow Chinese students, that is not a good outcome.

Participant: How unique is the concept and label of the accidental nation state?

Prof. Tan: Historically, many nation states emerged from decolonisation. The boundaries of many nation states were drawn arbitrarily by departing imperialists. Let me cite the example of South Asia, a region I have some knowledge of. The Indian subcontinent was very disparate before the British came and organised the whole area into a single territory. But when the British left, they carved out Pakistan, a new country that was divided into two wings. Can you imagine — one country, divided into two halves that are separated by almost a thousand miles? One wing subsequently became Bangladesh. For an island country like Singapore, the boundaries are clearer, but if you look at regions like Africa, the Middle East and South Asia, territorial boundaries were sometimes quite haphazardly decided. Even closer to Singapore, one might see Sabah's and Sarawak's entry into Malaysia, and Brunei's independence, as accidents of history. So I would say that we are not the only "unnatural nation". There are many others in the world.

Ms Lim: How does being an accidental nation state affect our process of national identity formation?

Prof. Tan: You have to work harder, as can be seen from the case of Singapore. Up to 1964 or 1965, the plan was to be a very successful city in the Malaysian Federation. But within 23 months of joining the Federation, Singapore found itself out on its own. An accidental and unnatural nation has to work doubly hard for its survival, and I think that was what Singapore went through in its first 20 or 30 years.

Participant: I am from Nation Builders. This year we intend to have the Singapore challenge on the hawker culture, so I would like to ask, what would be the next two major national challenges that you recommend we embark on?

Ms Lim: Could you tell us what is Nation Builders?

Participant: Nation Builders is a non-profit organisation that aims to encourage responsible and constructive citizenship. It is a ground-up movement that encourages Singaporeans to give back to society. We were incorporated last year.

Prof. Tan: I will give you one that is obviously very close to my heart — history. I think it would be a meaningful and interesting challenge for people to develop their own understanding of history and anchor their identities more deeply.

Let me cite the examples from a project I had mentioned in previous lectures.[1] We wanted young Singaporeans to develop stories that are important to them as individuals, as members of communities, and as a people.

We have 11 wonderful projects that are being showcased in a festival. One is an immersive production on resettlement and the Singapore Improvement Trust (now the Housing Development Board). I attended the production, a re-enactment of resettlement in the 1960s and 1970s, and experienced what it would have been like to be a resident, and have an officer explain what sort of compensation you would receive, based on your existing plot of land in the *kampung*.

Another project looks at how multiculturalism plays out on a personal level. The project creators are a Malaysian Sri Lankan Tamil young man and his girlfriend, who is an American-born Chinese. Both of them met in

---

[1] This refers to "The Future of Our Pasts" project, an arts and media festival organised by Yale-NUS College, from 16 February–17 March 2019.

Singapore and they have made a documentary film, called *Rojak Romance*.

A third project, a documentary titled *Merged*, relates to the merger of Tampines and Meridian Junior College, and what it means to people who are affected. A merger may be driven by practicality and function, but what is its significance for the people involved — the tuckshop owners, cleaners, long-serving teachers, students past and present?

These projects have explored the personal impact that history has on young Singaporeans, and I think this is important. Our personal connection to the past is something we must not lose. So, if you want a challenge, I would suggest getting more Singaporeans to find out and write about history that has meaning to them, from the ground up. There are lots of potential angles to explore, for instance, spaces — the market, schools, and streets.

Participant: An element of paramount importance in the journey of Singapore thus far has been the ruling party, PAP, in that it has consistently had a strong mandate to chart Singapore's journey. But at this point in time, with transition being on the cards, what are some pressing challenges for the administration moving forward?

Prof. Tan: The needs and aspirations of the younger generation. Lydia has written a wonderful piece, which I recommend, where she refers to an open letter written by a group of NUS students to the fourth Prime Minister.[2] The letter asks the political leadership: *Are you listening to us? Do you know what we want? Are you prepared to listen to dissenting voices without assuming we are simply disagreeing for the sake of it?* The new aspirations and needs of millennials are very different from those of previous generations.

The era of early nation building (1965 to 1985), and then sustaining

---

[2] Lydia Lim, "Identity in Singapore Version 4.0," in Commentary 27 — SGP 4.0: An Agenda, ed. Gillian Koh, 95–99 (Singapore: the National University of Singapore Society [NUSS], 2018), http://www.nuss.org.sg/publication/1548232969_commentary2018_Vol27_FINAL.pdf.

Singapore's success (late 1900s to the early 21st century), were characterised by different sets of challenges. In my view, how the government relates to a new generation of Singaporeans will be the main challenge moving forward.

Ms Lim: Perhaps younger Singaporeans would like to feel that they have a larger say in how the country is moving forward, and there is also the issue of whether we feel that the government trusts us enough to disagree while remaining patriotic to Singapore. I think that, as Prof. Tan said, there are changing expectations, and accordingly, there will be changing responses to new challenges that arise.

Participant: You said that national identity can be anchored upon historical memory, but I think our national identity is also borne out of certain erasures of our past. I was born in 1972 — all the schools I attended have moved or been closed down, and the spaces that I frequented as a teenager, like Far East Plaza, are no longer frequented by teenagers today. Likewise, the places my parents frequented, like Odeon and Cathay, were very different from the places my generation frequented. The only educational institution I attended that still exists in the same place is NUS, but it has undergone physical transformation too.

The rapidity with which our spaces change is unsettling. It has caused a rupture in our connection to the past, and in turn, our sense of national identity. What are your thoughts on this erasure of our past that takes place in the name of national progress and urban renewal? How can we anchor our national identity if we are continually losing spaces that remind us of our past?

Prof. Tan: This is the perennial challenge of a country that is also a city. Given our limited land area, in the name of progress, something has to give. We have the National Heritage Board (NHB), which looks into the preservation of monuments. They explore possibilities, but if you want to create new places for schools and housing etc., something has got to give because we do not have infinite space. So this is a trade-off that we have to deal with.

I agree that there is erasure, because when spaces are demolished or redeveloped, people often lose something familiar that they have grown up with. It is an issue that I do not have an answer to. I understand NHB is trying to find ways to engage communities, and enable individuals to take ownership of developing and preserving memories of spaces. I talked about the merger of junior colleges, that there is a sense of loss, and practical implications for staff who have to move elsewhere. But it is also possible to use technology to capture the sentiments and memories of students and staff in a school's final days, as seen from the documentary, *Merged*.[3] It is not ideal, but we can consciously preserve some of the memories of spaces, through ways besides physical preservation.

Ms Lim: Thank you very much, Prof. Tan, not only for the lecture, but also for your very passionate and candid responses. Some of the points you made really resonated with my own history.

---

[3] The documentary can be accessed here: http://merged.sg/

Lecture V

BEFORE NATION AND BEYOND
Places, Histories and Identities

Introduction

T oday, I would like to focus on the nature of nation states, identities and histories in Southeast Asia, including Singapore.

I will start by discussing a couple of key developments in the region that were instrumental in determining the shape of Southeast Asia as we know it today: these are the processes of decolonisation, and the consequent rise of nationalism and new states in the wake of European empires.

Decolonisation

Decolonisation is a critical facet of Southeast Asian history. Contemporary Southeast Asia emerged from colonialism and the imposition of the western concept of statehood and national frontiers.

The very idea of Southeast Asia as a region emerged from British strategic considerations during World War II. It arose from the "need to name a geographical entity on a map",[1] as a possible theatre of war. The term was then used to denote Mountbatten's Command in Colombo, which

---

[1] Russell H. Fifield, "Southeast Asia as a Regional Concept," *Southeast Asian Journal of Social Science* 11, no. 2 (1983): 1.

was called the South East Asia Command. The term became entrenched during the process of decolonisation, as the departing European powers came to think of the future of their colonies as a region.[2] It later became a Cold War construct.

Moving down from the regional level, the response of local populations and their respective leaders to departing colonial powers effected change across different countries. Nationalist organisations profited from the European loss of power to the Japanese during the War, and whether these nationalists cooperated with the Japanese (as Aung San and Sukarno did), or fought against all forms of colonialism (as Ho Chi Minh did), they fought for eventual independence from colonial rule.

While the colonial powers all wanted to regain their empires after the War, they knew that the post-war international climate and local conditions in their erstwhile colonies had changed. They were aware that they would not be returning to a power vacuum following the defeat of the Japanese. As the Japanese forces receded and European influence had not fully returned, the nationalists seized the moment and stepped into the gap.

The process of decolonisation varied throughout Southeast Asia. In Indonesia and Vietnam, the momentum of the revolutionary movements and the political and tactical weaknesses of the European powers brought about a relatively quick and bloody end to empire in the French and Dutch territories.

The British were able to delay the departure from their Southeast Asian colonies and achieve the outcomes they wanted — a peaceful transfer of power to local leaders who were prepared to keep their new states within the Commonwealth, with Myanmar (then Burma) being an exception.

The United States (US), which was allied with the British during World War II, tended to see the process of power transfer through the lens of the emerging Cold War. It was deeply suspicious of left-wing movements in the region, and while it had limited direct engagement in Southeast Asia, the US

---

[2] Ooi Kee Beng, "Southeast Asia and Foreign Empires," in *The Eurasian Core and Its Edges: Dialogues with Wang Gungwu on the History of the World* (Singapore: Institute of Southeast Asian Studies, 2014), 94.

had a major influence in the process of decolonisation. US policies alternated between the encouragement of gradual emancipation, and grander plans for development, regional stability and state building (in the image of the US). Like the European powers, the US affected the geopolitics of Southeast Asia, shaping identities that went beyond national boundaries.[3]

Nationalism and modern states

The end of World War II saw the rise of nationalism in different parts of Southeast Asia. Colonialism spawned the impulses for self-determination — first as resistance to colonial regimes, then as mass-based anti-colonial movements, uniting often disparate local populations with diverse concerns and grievances under the banner of nationalism, however vaguely defined.

Nationalism in Southeast Asia was for the most part generated by antagonism towards an alien and oppressive world order to which the local population had been subjected. However, as the ideas of nations and states were western modern concepts, they did not always sit well with local circumstances and polities in Southeast Asia. Still, nationalism as a political idea was domesticated by local elites — who had benefitted from a western education, which had in turn been used to co-opt them to serve the colonial system. These elites then used what they had learnt to perpetuate the ideals of community, self-determination and destiny for their own political purposes. Thus, as modern Southeast Asia emerged from the demise of the European empires, western ideas of statehood, national identity, democracy, territorial sovereignty and political boundaries were embraced as the natural order of things in a land that did not have any of these historical precedents.

With the emergence of states as the organising principle of the new world order, political frontiers, which were uncommon, if not unknown,

---

[3] Ronald W. Pruessen, Tan Tai Yong, and Marc Frey, *The Transformation of Southeast Asia: International Perspectives on Decolonization* (Singapore: NUS Press, 2003).

in the region were imposed on the political map of postcolonial Southeast Asia. This contrasted significantly with the old system, where the ambit of the state and structure of authority were determined by the power and influence wielded by the ruler. What counted in Southeast Asia was allegiance. Whom, rather than what, did the state comprise? The boundaries of states were rather inexact. Instead, "where the people went, there the state went."[4]

It was largely in the 19th and 20th centuries that frontiers and political boundaries took their current shape. In mainland Southeast Asia, agrarian systems had given a particular shape to states that had been in existence over some centuries. The Burmese, Thai, Vietnamese and Khmer states were recognisable entities before the Europeans determined their frontiers. The cultural characteristics that defined large proportions of their population, even though minority groups co-existed in their midst, persisted amidst the drawing of national boundaries.

Maritime Southeast Asia did not have the historical continuities of the agrarian-based polities of the mainland, and their frontiers were more decisively shaped by the Europeans. In these cases, political independence was not achieved through expressions of national identity that were predicated on cultural homogeneity, but through anti-colonial struggles and changes to the international order.

As a consequence, in maritime Southeast Asia, the state preceded the nation. Singapore and Indonesia are classic examples of this phenomenon. I have already spoken at length about Singapore in my previous lecture. The political scientist Benedict Anderson pointed out: "the 'stretch' of Indonesia ... does not remotely correspond to any pre-colonial domain ... its boundaries have been those left behind by the last Dutch conquests."[5]

As a result of these new frontiers, newly formed Southeast Asian nation states such as Myanmar, Indonesia, Malaya and Singapore faced challenges of

---

[4] Nicholas Tarling, *Nations and States in Southeast Asia* (New York: Cambridge University Press, 1998), 47.

[5] Benedict Anderson, *Imagined Communities* (London and New York: Verso, 1991), 120.

defining national identity amidst ethnic diversity. Many contemporary issues in Southeast Asia stem from these developments — Muslim separatism in the Philippines, Singapore-Malaysia relations, Burman majoritarianism. Even as there are tensions between competing ideologies and identities — ethnic, religious, national — there is also continued debate over shared culture and histories that transcend national boundaries (e.g., the evolution of *nusantara* as a concept, and the overlapping heritage of Singapore, Malaysia and Indonesia).

Dialogue with Professor Wang Gungwu

As a historian, I often delight in saying that the present cannot be understood without knowledge of the past.

It is therefore my pleasure to introduce my history guru and mentor, Professor Wang Gungwu, our foremost historian and world-renowned authority on Chinese and global history. I am deeply honoured to have Prof Wang join me in today's dialogue, on "Before Nation and Beyond: Places, Histories and Identities".

Professor Wang's experiences, where he lived and studied — in Malaya, China, Singapore and Australia — influenced and stimulated his views and deep understanding of the major changes that transformed Southeast Asia in the past 50–60 years.

Professor Wang is well positioned to offer insights on decolonisation and the rise of nation states in Southeast Asia, among other themes, and I am delighted to welcome him on stage.

Question-and-Answer Session

Transcript of Dialogue with Professor Wang Gungwu, moderated by Mr Janadas Devan

Lecture V was a departure from the usual lecture format. Following his brief remarks, Professor Tan Tai Yong was joined by eminent historian Professor Wang Gungwu in a dialogue. Professor Wang is Chairman of the ISEAS-Yusof Ishak Institute Board of Trustees. He is University Professor at the National University of Singapore and Emeritus Professor of Australia National University, a historian of China and Southeast Asia, and an authority on the Chinese diaspora.

Mr Janadas Devan: Prof. Tan has given a series of magisterial lectures, covering not only the history of Singapore, but the region, and Singapore's place in the region and the world.

The first generation of leadership in Singapore had not believed that the state of Singapore could exist without being part of a larger state that encompassed Malaya, in the first instance, and then, Malaysia. We could not have guessed it too, and it was not obvious when we became independent in 1965, that the equation that led us into Merger no longer paid. History took a surprising turn after 1965. 1965 — the Vietnam War was still raging, China had just begun to be engulfed by the Cultural Revolution, and the Cold War was ongoing. But, in retrospect, over the subsequent 50 years, we actually lived through a very long peace. Trade barriers fell, from the General Agreement on Tariffs and Trade (GATT), we got the World Trade Organization (WTO) and, as a result, partly by our own effort, but also because of a benign international situation, we became a prosperous state. Now, we might be seeing a reversal of all that. Will we be a nation that is able to withstand the challenges that globalisation in retreat may pose — both to the idea of nation states and to the idea of the nation?

Prof. Tan Tai Yong: I think Singapore will continue to flourish as a city-state, but whether it will continue to function as a nation state in the distant future remains an interesting question. Lee Kuan Yew asked that question at the end of his two-volume memoirs: what is going to happen two hundred years from now, and is Singapore going to survive in its current state. His answer was that Singapore will remain an island, but nobody knows if it will have longevity as a nation state.

Much will depend on the circumstances, but having built its identity and sovereign status over more than 50 years, Singapore the sovereign state is not going to go away easily. There will be struggles and challenges, but if we can embrace the ideas of rootedness and national belonging, and yet, continue to function as an open city-state — and Singapore has shown that it has the capacity to do so — then Singapore might do well. In a world where larger nations are closing up, Singapore could offer the alternative of a kind of nodal entity that can function in a more connected world. So I am optimistic, mainly because Singapore has shown its capacity to evolve and adapt over a period of history of much longer than 50 years.

Prof. Wang Gungwu: Well, I have a feeling that Tai Yong brought me up here to justify the title of his talk today: "Before Nation and Beyond: Places, Histories and Identities"!

The "before nation" part is obvious — I am older than him, and I have seen a lot more than he has. Indeed, I grew up with no sense of nation. I am old enough to have believed there was no such thing as nation. In the days when I became aware of nations coming to this part of the world, our identities were still linked up with our ethnicity — the language we spoke, our origins, where our parents came from. These were much more important markers of who you were than the idea of nations.

As late as the 1950s — depending on how you define "early" and "late" — there were many people in Singapore and Malaysia who really did not think of themselves as any kind of Southeast Asian nation, but still identified with their place of origins or where their parents had come from, be it China, India, Indonesia, or Thailand.

Now, I must say that all the words that Prof. Tan has used — identities, nations, states and so on, are all very difficult to pin down. They are very elusive and deceptive, and can be used in many ways to mean different things, and I have seen this done by different groups of people.

There is also another word that Tai Yong hinted at earlier, which I think is probably even more important. It is the background to what has happened, and the word is "empires".

This word is much more important than we realise because, in fact, empires were much more normal and were around for a long, long time. I am not just thinking of the ancient Chinese empire, the Roman empire, and the Persian empire. There is a whole list of old empires that had been around for very long. When we spoke of independence, anti-imperialism, anti-colonialism, we thought the age of empires had come to an end, and that they would be replaced by nation states.

My first awareness of the nation state was that it was something to replace all those terrible things called empires, which we had suffered under. We believed that the empires were the cause of our misery, and therefore, we had to get rid of the imperialists and have our own independent countries. All this was more or less believed by everybody.

For a long time, I too believed that the age of empires had come to an end. But the historian in me made me hesitate — for the simple reason that a lot of things seemed to change, but not change all that much. If ancient empires had been around for 4,000, 5,000 years, all over the Eurasian landmass, and in this part of the world, have they really gone away? Can something like nation states replace empires altogether?

I remember being very optimistic. I actually got up one day and stuck my neck out, and said, "Age of empires — over." But there were people in the audience who said, "Hang on, are you sure?" And that question remained in my mind for a while. I was pretty sure, but I am not so sure now.

"Empire" is another vague and difficult word. I always thought I understood what empire was, because I had lived through several. I was born in the Dutch empire; I grew up in the British empire; the Japanese came and there was the Japanese empire; then the British came back and there was the British empire; and then we had a new world order and the Cold War. One had the feeling that the world was divided into two empires — the communist empire and the capitalist empire — that was what the Cold War was about, the balance of power between two great conglomerations that behaved like empires.

Still, I put that aside, thinking the Cold War was just one grouping of nation states against another. But now, I am not so sure that the Cold War was not between two super empires, in a very different shape and form, grouping together in a very different way, unlike the old ways, where there had been colonies, armies and navies sent around, and the taking of other people's territories. In contrast, there was much more soft power. One sometimes gets the false optimism that soft power is really nice and soft and sweet, and all lovable and pleasurable. It is different from hard power, which is mainly linked to military power, and also political power, influence, and economic power.

But soft power is another form of power. It now takes the form of information, control of media, control of cyberspace, etc. Underlying this, is the extent of its control, how it controls, and how much it shapes the opinion of others, which reflects something that I would have called an empire in the past, although the empires in the past were much more crude and less subtle. I am now less confident that the age of empires is over.

In fact, in the last few years, I have become more sceptical that the age of empires is over. I have read about the battles over companies with artificial intelligence technology, robotics, the fantastic cyber and telecommunications systems that are being built up today, and the fact that all of us are exposed in some way or other. Even in Singapore, we were bewildered by the thought that we had been exposed to somebody who had gotten hold of our personal information. But what this boils down to is, are we sure that this is not something else that is operating, in a very different way, through soft and imperial penetration into our consciousness, and becoming part of us, even picking up things about us, in ways that are mysterious and unknown to us? I do not want to exaggerate this and alarm anybody, but I want to show that words like nations, empires, states, do not have a fixed meaning. They have a particular meaning at a particular point in time — at different times, they mean different things.

Even nation states meant different things for the Europeans in the days of the Treaty of Westphalia. When it first started, they were really not nations, but sovereign states. Some of those sovereign states became nations, and some did not. Some have actually been empires down to the present. Not only in Asia, but in Europe itself, the Austro-Hungarian empire, the Russian empire — large chunks of Europe were under imperial control until the 20th century.

So, when you look at it, empires have been long-lived and, until just a few decades ago, we had empires. So why were we so cheerful about the end of empires? At least I blame myself for being so innocent. So I am now putting it back to Prof. Tan, to say that the word "empires" is probably just as important as the three words that he has used in the title for today's lecture.

Prof. Tan: Maybe I should have added "empire". The point is, in this current international order, the state is the main player. Even in the era of empires, you had states. Whether it was the monarchy or the church, these entities functioned as states, controlling resources and people, and exercising influence or authority over territory.

But what you alluded to earlier was a fundamental change where the state need not be the key player anymore, because it is about control of information, and the main players could be companies or corporations, groups who control the Facebooks of the world. That would fundamentally alter the way in which the world might function in the future.

So, even if we use the word "empire" to mean a kind of order with a mix of different players, with one overarching authority, would it be possible to take away the state as a player, or would we see a world that is just a series of interconnected nodes of information control, where the critical points of the economy are being controlled by corporations, and not by states? The concept of nation states may not last, and a looser grouping of powers, whether they are hierarchically or laterally organised, may replace the current world order.

Mr Devan: Some months ago, Apple became the first company in history to reach the market capitalisation of US$1 trillion. That is larger than the Gross Domestic Product (GDP) of most countries. But to come back to your question, just as the death of empires might be much exaggerated, perhaps the nation state is somewhat more persistent than advertised. Even in history, the Treaty of Westphalia — at least in Western historiography — was supposed to be the beginning of the nation state. But if you go back further in history, some notion of the nation state must have existed as early as the 12th century in England, because you had maps that clearly demarcated England as a separate territory.

Even with the Treaty of Westphalia, you had principalities, German states, for example, that acquired sovereign status, only to be swallowed up later in a larger imagined nation state — Germany, which is really an empire. Even today, it is a collection of little German states.

In the 1990s, the term Washington Consensus was much bandied about, as supposedly the global consensus. Now the Washington Consensus is gone, and you have a regime in power that says, "America First". In Europe, just a few decades ago, the European Union was established, and it was supposed to have ended national boundaries in Europe, but, suddenly, you have Brexit, and Britain going its own way. So, the nation state is a persistent reality. Within Southeast Asia, we have not seen the emergence of an ASEAN community — if anything, it has taken a back seat.

Prof. Wang: Tai Yong is perfectly right — the state has persisted, in all its various forms — the kingdom, monarchy, city-states, nation states, imperial states. The state has existed as some form of organised structure and bureaucratic control, with the capacity to utilise all the technologies and tools available to control people, areas, their interests.

But how do you define the state, if the state itself takes different shapes? I am not suggesting that you can do away with the state, because no matter what kind of structure emerges, it requires people to lead, provide law and order, and enable people to live in peace, otherwise there would be constant barbarism. You can call these organised structures the state, and the state can take on many different forms. After all, when we started with tribal groups, you had the state. You had the leader and the state, the soldiers, and you could be very mobile and take over a lot of territory.

There is no question about the state's existence, in that abstract sense. We probably cannot do without the state. But whether the future state would be recognisable to us today, that I do not know.

Prof. Tan: I should quickly add that the East India Company became a state and an empire!

Prof. Wang: Nobody expected that! When the East India Company was founded, a bunch of merchants probably sat in a pub and thought, "What a good idea!"

Mr Devan: Now, let's have some questions from the floor.

Participant: My first question is, when the East India Company, or Raffles, founded Singapore in 1819, how important was the hinterland, in the 50 years thereafter? My second question is, if we take a look at the identity of Singapore today, how much of it would be a "Rafflesian identity", and how much of it would be a "Lee Kuan Yew identity"?

Prof. Tan: I have stopped using the word "founded" to describe the activity that led to the establishment of Singapore as a trading post in 1819. Raffles landed, he established a trading post, he bought over the island from the Malay sultan — well, it was John Crawford who sealed the deal. At that time, there was no physical hinterland. As I had said in my earlier lectures, the hinterland was actually sea-based. Raffles' interest in Singapore was related to maritime connections — he wanted to establish a foothold in the Straits of Melaka to protect the East India Company trade against the Dutch, and because India was already opening up and it wanted to trade with China — that was the kind of maritime passage that was important to control. So, the idea of a geographical hinterland up north did not feature in his calculations. It was more about the control of a strategic point for trade, and competition with the Dutch.

The second question was about identity. There was a group of people that basically had to establish a new state when Singapore had to exit Malaysia unexpectedly. It was led by Lee Kuan Yew, but he was not the only leader. The imprint of his leadership cannot be dismissed. How he envisioned Singapore to be disciplined, hardworking, resilient, able to make it on its own, yet open to exploiting the opportunities that were opening up around the nascent state, despite the fact that other opportunities were closed, all bore the imprint of the man, his ideas, his vision, and that of his team.

So I will not say that it was the work of Lee alone, but that he and his group of leaders had certain ideas about the new state and society they were trying to achieve. They were paternalistic, because they believed that strong leadership was critical. At that point, there was no nation to speak of. So there was nothing organic that was influencing the way Singapore would take shape. Leadership was imposed from the top, and therefore the imprint of Lee Kuan Yew and his fellow leaders was very prominent.

Prof. Wang: I would like to bring up a word that I have been talking about for some time. It originally stemmed from the idea that, when Singapore became independent it was a *unique* state. It became unique in the sense that Singapore was a totally unprepared state trying to build a nation. This uniqueness stems from the fact it was *separated* from Malaya, which Singapore had hoped to be part of.

Going back to Raffles, that same word, *separation*, came to my mind. Raffles separated a little island from the Johor empire, a Malay empire that had been there for a long time. Singapore was not only separate, it was in the middle of somebody else's empire, because the Dutch empire actually extended to the Malay Peninsula at that point too.

So, in the middle of it all, Singapore had to find ways of separating from the Malay empire, and from the Dutch empire, marking very clear borders between British and Dutch interests. In achieving that kind of difference, Singapore ended up being *unique*.

The first characteristic that makes Singapore unique is that it really was the only immigrant state in Asia that I know of. When it became independent in 1965, there were no other states in this part of the world that were almost purely made up of immigrants. You had migrant states in Latin America, North America, and Australasia, but they were very large entities, and they were really colonies, not a migrant state like Singapore. Singapore was a migrant city, a port city, with no plans to become a state.

This unique quality, of people coming from different parts of the world, basically meant that all the people who became citizens of this independent nation state had to separate from their own homes. It was not only a question of Singapore being separated from Malaya. All the people who became stakeholders on this island state also had to separate themselves mentally, if not psychologically and spiritually, from their connections.

It took them a long time. There are still people who are connected with their traditional homes and their places of origin, and the process of getting more people, in each generation, to separate from their homes, remains a work in progress. It is still part of the national programme, to make people separate themselves from their original homes. This was a tantalising thing to do, in the middle of other countries that were basically nativist, who believed that their natives should have priority, and that that was the basis for their nation state.

This is another intriguing part of Singapore. It is a very sensitive subject, but the fact was, when it started, it had a majority of people of Chinese origin, something like 75 per cent. The leaders succeeded in persuading this 75 per cent to not insist that they were Chinese or that this should be a Chinese state. I can still visualise some of the early leaders, going around trying to persuade the majority of their electorate not to see themselves as belonging to a Chinese state, but to this unique thing called Singapore. It was not an easy job.

Prof. Tan: Prof. Wang, can I ask you to elaborate on this point? Penang is another fascinating example. It did not end up like Singapore, a state on its own, it became part of the Malaysian state, but did it have other aspirations? There were many similarities between Singapore and Penang.

Prof. Wang: Well, they had no choice. I remember people in Penang asking not to be independent so that they could stay out of an independent Malaya, but they did not succeed. The British just parted from them.

Mr Devan: It is difficult to replay history, but it might have gone differently if, at that point in 1965, China was open. The Chinese in Singapore could not go back to China, because it was closed off then. And there was no Chinese immigration to Nanyang (South Seas); it had stopped with the People's Republic of China (PRC) in 1949. But even in 1965, in our narrative, we became independent in 1965, and suddenly, *fiat lux*, we created the idea of a new nation. Rajaratnam had been on record saying there is no such thing as a Singapore identity, and months later, he was asked to work on the Singapore pledge! So, it was an act of will that created Singapore.

Prof. Wang: And imagination too.

Mr Devan: Yes, and imagination. Speaking of imagination, you have said that you consider yourself a Malayan. Actually, so did almost everybody else in Singapore at that time. The word Singaporean did not exist. When the People's Action Party was inaugurated, it was Malayan nationalism, not Singaporean nationalism that was in its manifesto. And yet, curiously enough, though it was a very strongly imagined affiliation, historically, Singapore had never been ruled as part of Malaya. Singapore was ruled, for much of its existence, as a British colony, and together with Melaka and Penang, as a Straits Settlement.

After the war, it became a separate Crown Colony, because the British realised that the Malays would not accept a Malayan Union that included Singapore. So you had the Federation of Malaya, including Penang and Melaka (that is how Penang was separated from us), and Singapore as a Crown Colony. Yet, although we were never part of Malaya as an administrative entity, nevertheless, the strongest identity among the more educated segment of the population of Singapore, before 1965, was Malayan.

Prof. Wang: I was utterly astonished to find that Singapore was an independent nation, and utterly astonished at about the same time, that Malaya had disappeared. No Malaya now, it was Malaysia. Now, if you use the word Malaya, it is just a fantasy. I think most people do not know what Malaya means — I have discovered this in speaking to people, when, for instance, I say I had graduated from the University of Malaya …

Mr Devan: It still exists.

Prof. Wang: Yes — the Malaysian government has deliberately kept it, but made sure that it is a separate entity from their national university.

Mr Devan: That would be the Universiti Kebangsaan Malaysia.

Prof. Wang: It is extraordinary that Malaya has disappeared.

Participant: I wanted to pick up on Prof. Wang's characterisation earlier, of Singapore as a migrant state and migrant nation. In the last five to 10 years, we have seen currents that tend towards populist nationalism and xenophobia in our public discourse. Do these currents have their roots in forces in local politics, or further afield from Singapore?

Prof. Wang: This is definitely something in progress. Things are changing around us in ways that I certainly did not anticipate, and there are other possibilities that we cannot quite anticipate. For example, the whole regional and political structure, and the idea of one superpower controlling a single world order has now been questioned.

It was taken for granted for at least a couple of decades after the fall of the Soviet Union that the United States (US) would be *the* superpower that would police the world, and make sure that we all live happily together and so on. It has not worked out that way. Things have gone very wrong even in the eyes of American leaders themselves. They have not been able to prevent a lot of things from happening, and they now recognise that.

"America First" is not just nationalism, it is a kind of realism that they cannot do it by themselves, that they have to rely on a different kind of "soft imperialism", to bring out different sets of organisations and reorganise the world such that Americans, Chinese, Russians, Indians, Japanese can have control over different parts of the world.

Migration today, as compared to when our ancestors migrated, has changed. The kind of numbers that are involved, the kind of refugees going to Europe, the kind of migrations that people talk about. There are a hundred million migrants on the move, recently on the move or about to move right now. It is a different ball game altogether.

As for going "beyond nation", it is characterised by ease of communications and getting around, speed of movement, large numbers, and lack of control — I mean, poor US President Donald Trump is trying to build a wall! He is having great trouble within his own country, but the fact is that, no matter what he wants and likes to do, people are moving.

These are factors that I do not know how to build into the equations of the future. Are we really going to be able to hold our borders in the way we used to in the past? I am not sure, because when our ancestors moved, there were no borders to speak of. When I was a young boy, there was no such thing as borders. People spoke about the overseas Chinese being transnational in the days before there were nation states. Of course they were transnational — they did not even understand what a nation was!

To move around, all you had to do was have a pass to say that you had gotten a job — a labour agent had recruited you. A few hundred of them arrive, and they are just sorted out, declared to be healthy and clean and so on. That was about it. Nobody cared two hoots about your nationality and where you really came from, because everybody operated in that relatively very free world, moving — curiously enough — between different empires. As long as the empires' interests were protected, they could not care less where their labourers came from.

That was not that long ago. But I do not think we are going to have migrant states of that kind anymore. When you talk about new migrants, it is a different ball game. I am not sure if there are common factors uniting the different levels of workers that are coming into Singapore. I was astonished when someone explained to me the many levels and categories of work permits for them.

Mr Devan: Michel Foucault, I think, said that the state, to be a state, has to be able to do two things. One, control its borders, and two, control its population. So that is why we have so many grades of migrant labour.

There are some questions from the overflow room outside and from our online audience on Facebook. I will just ask each of you in turn. This one asks, do you see a day where companies such as Facebook, Apple or even Huawei, gain a certain degree of statehood?

Prof. Tan: I think they are going to be terribly influential, controlling economies, and flow of information, among other things. But whether they would be able to establish political control, I think that would require some stretch of imagination. I am not convinced that that will happen. But I think they will feature as significant players in the world system.

Mr Devan: There are some countries that are deploying diplomats to engage technology companies, the so-called digital ambassadors.

Another question from our online audience — how would the return of a Chinese empire look like?

Prof. Wang: Well, "Chinese empire" is another very interesting expression. The Chinese did not have a word for "empire". They used the word, *tianxia* (天下, literally "all under heaven"),[1] which does not translate as empire. They also had no sense of borders. If you look at the maps of all the dynasties of China, the borders were always changing.

There was a core group of people, but even then, there were times when China was occupied by non-Chinese people who conquered the whole of China. The idea of a Chinese empire which the Chinese talk about as if it has been continuous from the days of Confucius down to the present day, is based on an idea, which is not "empire" as we use it. The word "empire", derived from the word "imperium", was from the Roman empire.

The Chinese empire is not like the Roman empire at all. It is really a kind of civilisational state. It expanded its territory as more people became Chinese, assimilated or persuaded to become Chinese, or attracted by Chinese values and civilisation. As they grew and people on the borders of China accepted more and more ideas from the Chinese, they became part of China. Was that an empire? It is very hard to say.

For example, right now, the PRC has 55 minority groups, of which about four are very distinct and occupy large territories, like the Tibetans, Uighurs and the Mongols. These are the three largest. The other distinct group is the Hui, the Muslims. The Manchus had very large territory, and they have become totally Sinicised. However, the other so-called minorities are culturally distinct but they really have no national identity, and they are not unwilling to call themselves Chinese in a vague, cultural sense, unlike the Tibetans and Uighurs. The Han Chinese majority is probably recognised as the basis for the Han nationality, but the others, the 55 minorities, have very distinct characteristics of their own.

---

[1] Prof. Wang refers to the concept *tianxia* in his book, *Renewal: The Chinese State and the New Global History* (Hong Kong: Chinese University Press, 2013): "Some of China's rhetorical continuity came from the concept of *tianxia*, a vision of universality that was different from the idea of empire as exemplified in the Roman imperium" (p.132); "*Tianxia*, in contrast, depicts an enlightened realm that Confucian thinkers and mandarins raised to one of universal values that determined who was civilized and who was not. It is not easy to separate *tianxia* from the Chinese idea of empire because *tianxia* was also used to describe the foundation of the Qin-Han empire" (p.133).

One of the problems of calling China an empire is the fact that when standard empires break down, their people return home. When the Roman empire came to an end, the Romans all went back home to Rome, leaving behind a bit of France, a bit of Britain, a bit of Spain, and elsewhere. In the last hundred years, all the empires went home to their own nation states. But not China. The Manchu empire was definitely a Manchu and not a Chinese empire. The Manchu empire lasted for 250 years, but when it came to an end, they did not go home. They just became part of China. So that confuses us — what kind of an empire is that, when people have nowhere to go back home to? They were not a national empire to begin with. This creates a big problem, even today. The Chinese have tremendous difficulty in thinking of themselves as a nation. Every member of the United Nations is a nation state. But the PRC finds it extremely difficult to call itself a nation state. It is not a nation state. If anything, it is a multinational state.

Maybe India is the same. I like the way a great Indian diplomat answered, when asked the question of what was to be done about the Indian minorities. He said, in India, we are all minorities — everybody is a minority of one kind or the other. And when you think about it, he has a good point. But this is not true of China, which has a distinct Han majority.

Of course, if you visit China, you will find all these people who say, "We are Hokkiens, we are not like those Cantonese," etc. There are distinct local differences and people are very proud of these differences. But it does not stop them from thinking of themselves as part of the larger entity called China.

Whether that entity is actually a nation is another question, with its own set of problems. After they overthrew the Manchus in 1911, they created a republic called the Republic of China. They discovered that it consists of so many different peoples that they tried to invent a new nationality, *Zhonghua minzu*. But they have not been able to find out who is *Zhonghua minzu* till this day. This is not at all funny because the Chinese have tremendous difficulty convincing themselves that they are just another nation state, like Singapore, Denmark or Belgium. In fact, nations can be utterly different from each other, so that is one problem with the word nation. Who is a nation? What is the standard model of a nation state? I do not know.

Mr Devan: Just as the Manchus' empire disappeared but the Manchus remained part of China, the British empire disappeared but English became an Indian language and curry became an English dish, so identities are very fungible.

Participant: I have a question about the idea of the nation state and its continuation. With capitalism, you depend on law, trust, and contracts lasting for many years. The East India Company was very successful. It seems like that is locking us into a nation state structure, just because that has been such a successful strategy with regard to wealth creation across the world. Could I have your thoughts on that?

Prof. Wang: The gradations of nation states are, in fact, very considerable and varied. Some states quite readily became nation states because they were already homogenous. They were very nativist, they believed in ethnic community and unity, probably shared values, language, religion, and history that were clearly defined. Singapore is the other extreme, where you had to start from scratch to try and make everybody a Singaporean from 1965 onwards.

You will find that among nation states, some are very exclusive, closed and totally unwelcoming towards foreigners. On the other end of the spectrum would be nation states that are very open, but based on a completely different idea — the very modern idea of a civic state, as opposed to an ethnic state derived from bloodline, descent, kinship systems and so on.

A civic state is something you can join. It is like a club which you become a member of if you observe the rules and regulations. Now, that is pretty open and inclusive. It welcomes people whom it thinks can contribute. It is possible to form a nation state out of that.

In fact, all these definitions require a very strong commitment to law. Law defines certain things very sharply, and if you regard the law as sacred, are prepared to always go with the law, then you are one of us. That is also a nation, but there is a gulf between one extreme and the other. How these different nations relate to one another is one of the fascinating stories of the 20th century and we are still living it. I sometimes read some of the reports about the United Nations and I find it absolutely fascinating. Those 180 countries probably have 180 varieties of nationhood. To assume that they are all more or less the same and to expect them to behave in similar ways is folly, a complete misunderstanding of how they succeed.

Prof. Tan: But that is precisely the point, because the current world order is built on the fact that there are nation states that enjoy sovereignty, so, irrespective of its size, each is a player in the system.

Prof. Wang: An equal player.

Prof. Tan: An equal player, so Singapore has the same rights as the US or China in the international system. Unless the world order changes fundamentally, the idea of a sovereign nation state will persist, and no matter how you emerge, whether it is through a bifurcation of territory, or through independence from former empires, you have to acquire that status.

So, in 1965, when Singapore exited Malaysia, it had no choice but to be a nation state because that was the way the world was organised. The world order was structured around nation states, and that continues to be how states interact, how foreign policy is transacted.

In his book, *World Order*, Henry Kissinger talks about how the world order has evolved historically and reached this stage. I think the way he sees it is that it is going to stay, but then there will be all these tensions because nation states in the Middle East, Asia, Latin America and elsewhere function slightly differently. And there is no alternative at this point because of the way the world order exists.

Mr Devan: One should not underestimate the force and power of lived experience. In Singapore, we live in the same housing estates, men go through a certain common experience in the military. Frankly, I am surprised, looking back, at how rapidly we acquired the sense of being a Singaporean society.

Prof. Wang: It is surprising, but the uniqueness of that background remains. For Singapore, Separation in 1965 was a shock and a complete rethink that everybody had to go through. The fact that you wondered whether you could survive or not, and asked yourself what you had to do to survive — that was the experience of a whole generation.

I missed all that because I was not in Singapore, but my friends used to tell me how hard it was to think of themselves in this new state, because they never expected to be part of an independent state. But that very special experience is unique — to go back to the word "unique" again — that uniqueness cannot be reproduced anywhere else. It was a very special way of responding. And the swiftness with which you responded was because the pressure to adapt and rediscover yourself was so great. I do not think it normally happens in other countries.

Prof. Tan: We should perhaps go back to the earlier question about xenophobia. Out of a former colony, which then became for a short while a state in Malaysia, emerged a new nation state that needed to build an identity quickly. There was the need to build rootedness, give people a sense of home. When, in a way, Singapore succeeded in doing that, it created the sense that, since this is home, one is entitled to certain rights and privileges as a citizen of Singapore. When those privileges and rights are challenged because of competition from "outsiders", it generates xenophobia, a sense that foreigners are coming to take what is rightfully one's birth right. I think that partially answers the question.

We could do that when we have a stable population that continues to grow and continues to populate the state. But in our current situation and projecting into the future when the Singaporean core, which is born and raised here, starts to shrink in relation to the overall population, would the Singaporean identity that was built very quickly over 50 years persist, or would it be diluted? One way, then, might be to go back to the old formula where Singapore has to be an open global city; you have a small group of people who call themselves citizens, some are new citizens, but one-third or more of your population could be transient workers moving in and out. This will certainly have an impact on Singapore as a nation state.

Participant: Prof. Wang mentioned just now that Singapore is unique in the sense that we are all basically immigrants. I do not know how Malays might feel about that kind of statement. When we celebrate our Bicentennial, there will be a book on the Bicentennial from the Malay perspective. We are happy that the government has chosen the approach that it is not just about Raffles but will go beyond Raffles; although we are celebrating our Bicentennial, we are going further back to 700 years. I recall a letter in *The Straits Times* saying, when you talk about history, will it be the Malays or do we go beyond the Malays, which means Srivijaya and the others?

Prof. Wang: History is, in one sense, very simple. There is history, meaning the past — whatever happened, we do not know, and we try to find out what in fact happened. Then there are other histories, which are actually man-made, maybe by the historian, a government, a ruler, or a dictator. The victors certainly wrote the histories; the people who lost had no chance to write the history. These are the histories in the books that we read, which are written by people, usually with an agenda of one kind or another.

Now, the professional historian who believes that he should try and find out what really happened belongs to a very rare group of people. Most of their books are not read by anyone, because they try so hard to prove one thing or the other! You cannot follow them because it is very difficult, the evidence is never clear-cut, and there are lots of controversies among professional historians.

But the historian who writes a popular book with a very clear angle that fits your picture of the world — that, you can absorb very quickly. And from this point of view, governments find it irresistible to rewrite history. I am saying this of all governments, not just the Singapore government. In fact, I honestly do not know of any national history that did not have an agenda, a government agenda, behind the national history directly or indirectly, subtly or more crudely. They want a particular story to be told for a particular reason at a particular time. At a different time, they — probably the same people — might tell it differently. But certainly, at different periods of time, people rewrite their own history. All countries rewrite their history. Even today, we are rewriting a lot of the history that we had learned as students in school. Because the perspective changed, our interest changed; we are looking at different frameworks and the whole world order as it shifts. This influences the way we look at history, so history is elusive and difficult to deal with, but this is inevitable.

Prof. Tan: We tend to assume that history is always finite and final. This is not true. And what we should be more interested in is the writing of history — as an enterprise or an exercise. Take the example of the Bicentennial — that is an exercise in history writing or understanding history. So then, do you start at 1819 or do you start further back? What do you include, and what do you exclude? I think this is where space has to be created, not just for the state to have a say in the history of the country or people, but to have a variety of voices so that you can have an enriched understanding of the very complex process of history writing. This is something we hope will happen, and I have always argued that, in marking the Bicentennial, it should not just be a state-directed effort that is forgotten after 2019 passes by. It should spark a renewed interest and curiosity in the history of our past, the history of various groups that came before the Europeans, made Singapore their home, and developed Singapore as a port city.

Participant: Given that our conception of a Singaporean identity has evolved quite rapidly over five decades, in the age of technology, social media and greater information flow, will this speed up? For instance, Singaporeans had quickly rallied online in defence of Singapore in recent incidents involving Malaysia.

Participant: Can you foresee the youth of today preserving historical cultures and traditions in the era of exponential change, where different cultures fuse to form new identities in an interconnected world?

Prof. Tan: This is linked to the previous question of history writing and understanding history. The state plays a very prominent role in creating that narrative. You have to create a narrative to get people to believe that this is the trajectory: this is where we come from, and this is where we will go. You have to give them hope that the trajectory will always be a positive one. But history is going to be more complex moving forward. It is going to require more effort and many more people writing their histories, their part in the national story of Singapore. Social media will further open up the space and provide opportunities for young people to engage in historical conversations. In the past, if you did not attend a history class or attend a talk like this, you would most probably not engage with history. This has changed with social media, making it all the more important for serious historians to listen to the multitude of voices, and to try to incorporate as many of these voices as possible in their own historical interpretation.

As for the point about cross-cultural interactions, yes, it is no longer the history of one people, one state, within clear boundaries; it is going to be very mixed now. If I were to write the history of Singapore 50 years down the road, it would be a very different sort of history from the kinds of history that we are used to seeing, written in the 1960s and 1970s. It is going to evolve and change. But this is what makes history exciting and alive — it does not simply end at a certain point. It is not the case that all the histories have been written and there is nothing more to say. This is why having young people engage in this enterprise is very important. Creating space for this plurality of views will be just as important.

Prof. Wang: I want to go back to the word "state" that Prof. Tan insisted was a very crucial part of our society. I think what history shows — in all the history that we can read, regardless of who writes it — is that, in the end, some states succeed and some states do not. The failed states were the badly governed ones, with incompetent or tyrannical leaders. Whereas the states that are governed by well-trained professional people committed to providing good governance and so on, succeed. This is actually taught by history. A successful state depends on what we call good governance, tends to have committed people who are prepared to work very hard to ensure that the state functions well, makes progress, and enables most of its people to be happy and content — all very difficult ideals. But those who are capable of achieving some part of that deserve to be recognised as a successful state.

Mr Devan: I am afraid I have to bring this to an end. Today's dialogue between these two distinguished historians serves as a demonstration of what historical thinking really means and entails.

Lecture VI

WHAT TO DO WITH HISTORY?

Introduction

This is my sixth and final lecture of the series. In previous lectures, I explained how Singapore was shaped by forces of early globalisation and the continuities that underlie Singapore's position as an open port city constantly searching for hinterlands.

In this long narrative, stretching over 700 years, Singapore's current status as a nation state appears but as a short blip. Will Singapore endure as a nation state, even as it reverts to its traditional instincts as a globally oriented port city that needs to stay open and connected to thrive? Where are we in the latest cycle of history and what sort of future can we anticipate?

Since 1965, Singapore has always been a forward-looking nation state. It has tried to anticipate problems and stay ahead of the curve. This is of critical importance to a young city-state that does not have a civilisational and cultural core or a natural hinterland, and whose destiny has always been tied to larger forces beyond its shores.

Even as we look forward, it is important to understand that our current situation is always the result of preceding events, and that we are shaped by the circumstances, choices and actions of the past. Therefore, we cannot understand our present situation without knowing history, much as progress cannot be made by constantly looking at the rear mirror.

As I mentioned in my first lecture, there was the sense, by the 1980s, that young Singaporeans had lost touch with their history, and there was a need to introduce national education to promote an appreciation of the challenges we had faced in the past, where we had come from, and how we got here. This would then hopefully give us a better sense of how we should manage the present and can perhaps plan for the future.

In this lecture, I intend to discuss how we can better understand and appreciate our history. Is merely knowing what happened in the past sufficient? I will argue that having historical knowledge provides a necessary foundation. But, to truly understand what history means and how it affects our personal and public lives, we need to develop a deep sense of historical consciousness and cultivate our capacity for historical imagination.

How well do we know our history?

Singaporeans are generally aware of the official "Singapore Story". This is taught in our schools, featured in the biographies of political leaders, performed in our National Day Parades, and exhibited in our national museums. Because of this exposure, Singaporeans may think that they already know all there is to know about Singapore's history, from colonialism, war and occupation, to political change and independence.

Singaporeans are also aware of the broad history of the region, and key pivotal world events like World War II. Their historical knowledge can be seen from the results of a pop quiz on Singapore history, conducted by *Channel NewsAsia* (CNA) last year. Among its interviewees, CNA found that younger Singaporeans between the ages of 20 and 40 did better on the quiz.[1] This is not surprising as Singaporeans, especially those who

---

[1] Fann Sim, "Going Beyond 1819: How Well Do Singaporeans Know the History of Singapore?" *Channel NewsAsia*, February 17, 2018, https://www.channelnewsasia.com/news/singapore/going-beyond-1819-how-well-do-singaporeans-know-the-history-of-9945420.

went to school in the 1990s onwards, have been exposed to national education and compulsory social studies, which included history, in the school curriculum.

But history is more than the official Singapore narrative. This is not to say historical knowledge imparted through state institutions (like schools and museums) is not important. The overarching narrative — the way in which the official history is written — provides a frame and a chronology with which to make sense of the series of events that resulted in Singapore becoming what it is today.

Without this narrative structure, we would not have a coherent history of the nation state. But how do we make our history relatable to us as individuals or members of a community? And is the national narrative the final word? Or is there more to our history than what we have learnt in schools and through state institutions?

The importance of historical consciousness

Knowing and appreciating key facts of the past does not necessarily make history personally relevant or meaningful. We often hear the lament that history is dry and boring, a school subject that students have to study to pass examinations, and worse, nothing more than propaganda. Beyond historical literacy — that is, knowing what happened, it is crucial to develop what I call historical consciousness, which is the ability to make the past have meaning for us as individuals and as communities.

It is also the ability to understand why things happened. In other words, historical consciousness allows us to develop individual and collective understandings of the past, and to be aware of the cognitive and cultural factors that shape those understandings.

Historical consciousness rests on collective memories. Collective memories are the shared memories and knowledge of a social group. These memories are used by the group to interpret a past that resonates with how they identify themselves. For example, the Chinese people remember the period from 1839 to 1949 as the "century of humiliation", during which China was bullied and humiliated by foreign powers. This powerful collective memory influences the way China conducts itself in world affairs today. Sometimes, these collective memories are framed as part of present developments, rather than the past.

Many younger Singaporeans may find historical consciousness difficult to achieve because they lack the lived memories that earlier generations have — some painful and frightening, others bittersweet or exciting. Historical consciousness has been eroded by collective forgetfulness, as direct links to an immediate past have been replaced by an orientation towards change and progress.

Singapore's rapid development in the last 50 years has challenged the different ways people bind themselves to their community and country. Experiencing constant change in our physical and social environments can leave precious few things that yield sufficient attachment and endearing familiarity to people. Memories fade when traces of the past start to vanish. We cannot take for granted that the physical embodiments of our history, elements of our collective memories, will always be here to stay. To return to an earlier lecture, someone in the audience raised the question of how we can anchor national identity in the face of continual loss of physical spaces such as places of worship and schools, and the resulting erasures of our past. My response was that anchoring national identity to physical embodiments of memories and heritage remains a perennial challenge for a small city-state like Singapore. There is a tension between pursuing progress and efficient land use, and preserving physical spaces that people deem to be of historical and cultural value.

Monuments in Singapore of historic, cultural, symbolic significance etc. and national importance have been protected by the Preservation of Monuments Board, later renamed the Preservation of Sites and Monuments (PSM), a division under the National Heritage Board.[2] Separately, the Urban Redevelopment Authority (URA) has done its part to preserve

---

[2] Melody Zaccheus, "The Balance Between National Progress and Preservation of Heritage," *The Straits Times*, May 6, 2019, https://www.straitstimes.com/opinion/the-balance-between-national-progress-and-preservation-of-heritage.

old buildings in its land use planning. While these attempts, sometimes promoted by civic activism, have been laudable, it is not always possible to keep things unchanged due to Singapore's limited land area. Still, there is no disputing that heritage sites "add value to the landscape and provide a sense of familiarity, place and time, rooting the people of Singapore to their homeland."[3]

Perhaps we have to seek alternative ways of developing and preserving memories of spaces. Let me give the example of *Merged,* a documentary on the merger of two junior colleges (JCs), Tampines JC and Meridian JC, that was produced as part of "The Future of Our Pasts". The documentary tries to capture, through digital means, the sentiments and memories of students and staff in the schools' final days before merger. Digital preservation of memories as opposed to physical conservation of places may not be ideal, but it is still a way of preserving memories.

Historical consciousness happens when there is personal resonance with the past. This often has a deep influence on perceptions of and reactions to the way history is remembered through public events. A good example was an exhibition gallery on the Japanese Occupation at the Former Ford Factory. Originally, the gallery and exhibition was named "Syonan Gallery", to reflect the name that the Japanese gave Singapore under the Japanese Occupation. It had negative connotations, but the curators argued that referencing "Syonan" was a way of remembering a painful chapter in Singapore's past and Singapore's vulnerability.

However, following public outcry from others who saw the name "Syonan Gallery" as inappropriately glorifying the occupation, the exhibition and gallery was renamed "Surviving the Japanese Occupation: War and its Legacies". The latter group may have been a loud minority, but this incident revealed the importance of taking into account the different feelings and significance that various groups in society attach to a single historical event. In this instance, the majority of society might have had

---

[3] Ibid.

no opinion, or were emotionally and intellectually prepared to move on. But there were people who still had painful memories of that period and it was necessary to respectfully validate those sentiments and connections to the past.

Historical consciousness can be enhanced when we take ownership of our histories, and not allow our historical inheritance and collective memories to erode with time. But people have also said that Singapore is historically sterile; all we have is ultra-modernity and history is being lost in the name of progress. I am not sure if I agree with this sentiment. Thanks to the efforts of the National Heritage Board, you will find that history is actually all around us. As such, taking time to pause and read commemorative plaques and signs that display historical information is one step we can all take to appreciate the history around us. Few people know that the hawker centre at Tiong Bahru was probably the first such centre to be paid for by the hawkers themselves. In a grand collective action, these previously illegal or itinerant hawkers got together, negotiated with the government, and raised an infrastructure that was later redeveloped into the two-storey building seen along Seng Poh Road today. This is not a piece of history we find readily in our history books, or even on the signs in front of Tiong Bahru market, but it is a true Singaporean story.

For the more internet savvy among us, the website Roots.sg, run by the National Heritage Board, maps out heritage trails, monuments, historical site markers, and buildings and sites, among other material. It also documents Singapore's national collection, allowing users to view images and other information relating to artefacts. This resource, which was launched in 2016 and is publicly accessible, is one way we can explore Singapore's history in our own time. There is also an abundance of materials in the National Library and National Archives. Among these materials are stories of the past, told from individual perspectives, which can make history come to life, with the potential to evoke sympathy and emotional resonance.

One example is the story of a man, Mr Yap Yan Hong, who miraculously escaped being killed at Changi Beach during Operation Sook Ching. His oral history can be found on Archives Online. Here is an excerpt of his recount:

> *There were three groups — 18 of us. Three soldiers. It was then that we began to worry as to what would happen. So, one of the captives in the group asked the Japanese soldiers, "Master, ini mana pergi?" He spoke in Malay. Then the soldier replied, "Sana itu go, san tien kok, kok, kok, okay." In other words he meant that he would be retained [sic] for three days chipping rocks and we would be released.*
>
> *So, we thought that our destination would be Changi Prison because the lorries were heading towards Changi Road. Then after when we passed Changi Prison and the lorries didn't stop, we began to have more worries. We were imagining all sorts of things. And our hands were tied behind our back, our knees were tied and they were so tight that blood circulation began to affect us. And we were telling ourselves that they were really going to shoot us, they were really going to kill us. Because the man said we would stop somewhere near the Changi Prison, chip stones for three days and then we would be released…*
>
> *So, I swam and swam until I was so tired. I said, "Well, this is the time I drown." I told myself that. So, I just allowed myself to go down, both my feet touched bottom and then believe me or not my nose was just above water. When I looked back it was around about 600 yards from the shore. I say 600 yards because I know the distance. During our manoeuvring days we used to go for shooting practice and 600 yards is about that distance.*
>
> *So, when I looked back at the shore it was about 600 yards. It was then that I heard a whistle, an ordinary whistle. And somehow or other it clicked on my mind, this is when the firing*

would start and actually after the whistle the machine gun
opened up, you see. I took a deep breath and went under water
and I could hear the bullets ricocheting above me. I never knew
what a ricocheting bullet sounded like and that was the first
occasion I heard it. It went zioong, zioong, zioong *above water.*[4]

Here, Yap was describing his thought process when he and other
men were brought onto a lorry by a Japanese soldier, and then how he
managed to stay undetected as the shooting started. There is a treasure
trove of material, be it compelling anecdotes or intriguing artefacts, which
exist in the public domain and are essentially at our fingertips. If we are
serious about historical consciousness, these are materials we can use, to
build our knowledge and aid our exploration and imagination of the past.

The next point I would like to make about historical consciousness is
that it is not just an intuitive feeling or a memory. Historical consciousness
requires a degree of intellectual rigour, and open-mindedness in seeking to
understand why decisions were made. It goes beyond simply asking "what
happened", to questioning "why it happened". To understand why things
happened, it is important to appreciate contexts and nuance. History does
not always progress in a straight line, and our present and future can be
shaped by unexpected contingencies and twists.

The centrality of context

Historical actions and events do not happen in isolation; the environment
in which things happen and the circumstances of the time often shape and
determine why and how decisions and actions are taken. Understanding
contexts is a good antidote to the inappropriate application of
hindsight. Understanding the culture, collective mentality, and physical,

---

[4] "Oral History Interview of Yap Yan Hong (Singapore, 1989)," Oral History Interviews, National Archives of
Singapore, http://www.nas.gov.sg/archivesonline/oral_history_interviews/record-details/99c30aa3-115f-11e3-83d5-
0050568939ad?keywords=yap%20yan%20hong&keywords-type=all. The audio recording for these excerpts are at
19:23–21:22 and 26:57–27:30, respectively.

technological and geographical environment in which things happen allows us to interpret and understand events and actions in the time and place that they had occurred, rather than merely judging them by contemporary standards, or worse, in accordance with our own beliefs and prejudices. We appreciate things better when we do not impose our own lenses and perspectives in understanding past decisions. We cannot assume that historical actors had the privilege of knowing what the future held when they made the choices of their times. Their choices and options were necessarily limited by the realities of their immediate contexts. Let me offer an example.

On May 13, 1940, Winston Churchill made his first speech in the House of Commons, announcing that he had "nothing to offer but blood, toil, tears and sweat." He pledged himself to a policy of waging war "by sea, land and air", with the single aim of "victory at all costs, victory in spite of all terror, victory, however long and hard the road may be."[5] This short speech is now regarded as a turning point, an iconic moment in the history of the War. It would be easy to believe, hearing that speech now, that Britain had turned the corner and was on its way to defeating the Nazis.

But this view is coloured by hindsight and by our knowledge that Britain and the allies would emerge victorious from the War. Was this apparent to Churchill and his audience at the time? Obviously not. Churchill and many members of his Cabinet understood then that the options were limited. Britain had its back to the wall; it could choose to compromise or to show defiance and fight even though the odds of victory were not good. Churchill chose the latter, and many of his critics thought him reckless and foolhardy at that time. In the short term, Britain was about to enter into its darkest hour. And Singapore would fall less than two years after that speech.

Understanding contexts allows a historical figure to predict the likely

---

[5] Winston Churchill, "First Speech as Prime Minister to House of Commons (Blood, Toil, Tears and Sweat)," The International Churchill Society, May 13, 1940, https://winstonchurchill.org/resources/speeches/1940-the-finest-hour/blood-toil-tears-and-sweat-2/.

consequences of her proposed action. It also enables the historian to explain the actual consequences. The historical figure can never be certain of the future — at best, she can only deal with probabilities.

Capriciousness of contingencies or chances

Many of you may have heard of the assertion that if Cleopatra's nose had been shorter, the course of western history would have been different. Human affairs are unpredictable and events do not proceed on predetermined trajectories. Sheer chance and contingencies can be powerful forces in determining outcomes in history.

Histories that are used to project progress and advancement tend to underplay or ignore the role of chance. This is true of some historians with Marxist or religious persuasions, or those who may be overly influenced by certain theories. They tend to believe that events follow a pre-determined course which allows them to foresee the future. But we all know that the unexpected happens, and at each critical point in our past, the historical trajectory could have taken an unexpected turn, caused by force of personality or unanticipated circumstances. Let me give an example:

In the 1950s, Singapore could not envisage a future without the Malayan hinterland. The People's Action Party (PAP) government made merger with Malaya its election manifesto in 1959, and after a bout of acrimonious negotiations with its Malayan counterparts, Singapore became part of Malaysia in 1963. In the process, the PAP split and the left-wing leadership was decimated. Everyone at that point in time thought that the deed was done, and Singapore had found its rightful place within the Malaysian nation.

But, troubles soon followed and relations between Singapore and Kuala Lumpur started to worsen. The strained relationship became untenable when the ideological differences between the "Malay supremacy" that certain UMNO leaders were committed to and a "Malaysian Malaysia" promoted by Singapore leaders came to a head. So, despite the efforts and desires that led to Merger, the marriage broke up within two years. On 9 August, 1965, Singapore proclaimed its independence, officially leaving Malaysia. Did Lee Kuan Yew and his colleagues expect this to happen in September 1963? Probably not.

While history may be necessary for nation building purposes, it is also a powerful device that can give meaning to our personal identities. Personal and shared historical experience is an important marker and maker of identity. Having a strong sense of historical consciousness will not only give us a better appreciation of our identities, it would help us to understand what makes and holds us together as a community and a country.

Expanding our historical imagination

It is not enough to have historical consciousness. We also need historical imagination in our writing and understanding of history. What do I mean by historical imagination? The imaginary does not have to be unreal. Historical imagination has to do with the ability to offer new ways of thinking about past events, to not only examine the observable, but also find clues and traces of the unobservable (such as thoughts and motivations behind certain actions). How does one, for example, write the history of an event or group of people for which there are limited primary sources and written documentation? This was something the Subaltern School historians had to contend with when writing about peasant uprisings in British India from the perspective of the peasants.

In 1857, the British colonial state was nearly overthrown by a mass mutiny of Indian sepoys (soldiers) of the Bengal Army. The British would explain that the soldiers had mutinied because of unhappiness with the terms of service, and it was weak and insensitive military leadership that had led to the eruption of the mutiny. But, as historians investigated further, it became evident that the mutiny by sections of the Bengal regiments was merely the spark that eventually triggered a broad-based revolt by different sections of Indian society, whose lives had been adversely affected by the imposition of colonialism. Ultimately, it was a revolt involving not just sepoys, but also peasants, landlords and princes, motivated by different specific interests, but driven by common grievances against colonialism. If not for the historical imagination of the historian, the complexities and widespread effects of what was euphemistically called the Indian Mutiny would never be fully understood.

Moving to another mutiny closer to home, I would like to mention the work of Nurfadzilah Yahaya on the Sepoy Mutiny in Singapore in 1915. The colonial archive on the event is focused on the government and army command. How then, does one write the history of the Sepoy Mutiny from the perspective of the soldiers?

Dr Yahaya's research looks at sepoy testimonies recorded verbatim by British officers in the aftermath of the Mutiny as well as nine letters that were intercepted and translated, which offer rare insight into the motivations of the soldiers and their views on their military postings. Through these transcripts and testimonies, one gets a palpable, poignant understanding of the soldiers' sense of isolation as they are subjected to what Dr Yahaya describes as "a life of circulation without mobility." An interesting point she noticed in the Commission of Enquiry report issued after the 1915 mutiny was the frequent mention of "going towards Singapore" by the sepoys even though they were, in fact, stationed on the island. Local civilians were reportedly puzzled by the soldiers' requests for directions to Singapore. The term "Singapore", Dr Yahaya suggests, seemed to have referred to the urban core of the island even though its geographical contours were never defined by any sepoy. This reinforces Dr Yahaya's argument that the soldiers were kept apart from the rest of Singapore, displaced and disconnected from the environment they were supposed to guard and protect.[6]

Historians are constantly pushing the boundaries of historical knowledge. The discipline expects this of them, and efforts at revising

---

[6] Nurfadzilah Yahaya, "Alternate Pasts: Politics of Commemoration of 1915," presented at "The Future of Our Pasts" festival, Singapore, February 27, 2019.

history and adding to existing historical knowledge should be welcomed. This is where historical imagination comes in. It involves employing creativity in interpreting sources (archival documents, legal documents, oral history interviews, etc.) and coming up with new analytical frameworks, all while remaining within the perimeters of evidence-based historical context.

But let us not forget that historians are storytellers too. They craft narratives in an attempt to make sense of what happened. One of the marks of good historical scholarship is the combination of careful documentation with artful construction. Good history is rigorous, critical and compelling. People should ideally want to read it, find out more about it, and be excited by it. How else can history be educational, relatable and relevant?

Just recently — from February to March — Yale-NUS College ran a month-long history-and-art festival in conjunction with the Singapore Bicentennial. Project creators were encouraged to examine less explored aspects of Singapore history and present their research findings using artistic, creative mediums. We wanted young Singaporeans to write their own history and, in doing so, develop a sense of belonging and identity. Eleven projects by students and recent graduates from different tertiary institutions in Singapore were selected for the festival. During the year and a half following the open call, the teams refined their ideas and projects through a series of workshops and critique sessions attended by artists, writers, curators and academics.

For some project creators who were undertaking a creative project for the first time, it was a journey of learning and discovery. Through the process, they became aware of the complexities of history writing and the act of constructing a narrative. Through the works, we encounter personal histories, community histories, and histories of places gone and places still in existence. We encounter stories told by young people in Singapore, of love, loss, self-discovery and identity — stories we can all relate to in some way. Each project provided different entry points for audiences to "reimagine" Singapore's history, through performances, exhibitions, public installations, books, films, and a web-based interactive documentary. In addition, fringe programmes including film screenings, walking tours, talks and panel discussions were also organised to encourage conversations about history.

There is *Boka di Stori*, a graphic novel which brings to life the history and culture of the Eurasian community in Singapore. The title of the graphic novel is a Kristang phrase that translates into English as "mouth of stories"; it also means "storyteller". A large part of the project involved the creators speaking to members of the Eurasian community to collect stories and materials for the novel. Personal histories matter as much as broad historical narratives.

Another history-based graphic novel I would like to mention is *The Art of Charlie Chan Hock Chye* by Sonny Liew. I am sure many of you are familiar with Liew's work, which has been described by a reviewer as "an ambitious, innovative work." What makes this work distinctive, especially from a historical perspective?

The Art of Charlie Chan manages to move seamlessly, unhampered, between fact and fiction. Liew spent a lot of time on research in his retelling of historical events in Singapore. We see this in the extensive footnotes and sources. But he also turns evidence on its head, and subverts methods used traditionally by historians working within conventional academic settings to establish veracity: photographs, newspaper clippings, etc.

We can reasonably conclude that the author is challenging us not to take any text and narrative for granted. The success and popularity of *The Art of Charlie Chan* in Singapore and Malaysia demonstrates that the medium of the comic book, like other artistic approaches to historical narratives, allows us to expand our historical imagination. It makes history accessible outside of academic settings, and can generate an openness and growing appetite among Singaporeans for new interpretations of history.

Conclusion

As Singapore develops as a country, it is critical for us to have a deeper, more inclusive and more nuanced appreciation of our history and heritage. This should not be driven solely by the state, in the form of national education; we should also encourage bottom-up, community-led efforts so that history becomes an organic, shared and inclusive force in the making of national identity.

Why is history important? Because it "allows us to fulfil our need for self-examination and awareness … so that what is needed is a study of how we came to be the sorts of people that we are, of why we have the perceptions, the outlooks and the attitudes that we have."[7]

Personal and shared historical experience is an important marker and maker of identity, and having a strong sense of historical consciousness will help us make sense of what makes and holds us together as a community and a country. Historical imagination comes into play here as well. We weave past events, interactions and individuals into a comprehensible narrative.

Historical consciousness and imagination also means being open to nuance and accepting complexity. "We … tend to simplify history: but the pattern within which events are ordered is not always identifiable in a single unequivocal fashion, and it may therefore happen that different historians understand and construe history in ways that are incompatible with one another …"[8] Not all frameworks are equally plausible, but historical imagination should mean the possibility of different ways of seeing.

Edward Luce, a British journalist, recently wrote an article in the *Financial Times,* making a case for the relevance of history. History is decreasing in popularity, while fields like science, technology, engineering and mathematics (STEM) are seen as paths to economic success. However, while we may rely more on algorithms and automation today, it is still up to us as individuals to discern, judge and be well-informed so that we

---

[7] Beverley C. Southgate, *History: What and Why? Ancient, Modern, and Postmodern Perspectives* (London, New York: Routledge, 1996).

[8] Primo Levi, *The Drowned and the Saved* (London: Abacus, 1989), 22–23.

do not fall prey to civic ignorance, fake news and other phenomena that may divide us. As Luce puts it, "a well-informed citizenry … creates a stronger society. We may no longer be interested in history, but history is still interested in us."[9]

Let me end with a quote by Henry Kissinger, who in his book, *World Order,* made the following observation: "Long ago, in youth, I was brash enough to think myself able to pronounce on 'The Meaning of History'. I now know that history's meaning is a matter to be discovered, not declared. It is a question we must attempt to answer as best we can in recognition that it will remain open to debate."[10]

---

[9] Edward Luce, "US Declining Interest in History Presents Risk to Democracy," *Financial Times*, May 2, 2019, https://www.ft.com/content/e19d957c-6ca3-11e9-80c7-60ee53e6681d.

[10] Henry Kissinger, *World Order* (New York: Penguin Press, 2014), 374.

Question-and-Answer Session

Moderated by Professor Kwok Kian Woon

Professor Kwok Kian Woon: Thank you for a most insightful lecture. I must say we all enjoyed the fascinating examples you used to make your points more concrete.

You spoke about painful and traumatic memories. Almost every country has such memories — Indonesia with the events of the mid-1960s; Cambodia with the genocide; and China with the Cultural Revolution. Singapore may have some of these memories, going back to the days of decolonisation and early nationhood. It seems to me that when we revisit and reflect on those past events, we are not just trying to remember the past, or reconcile our relationship with it. There is also a component of imagining the future. I think this might be what you are indicating. Perhaps there is a tension between ideals for what that desired future might be and limitations drawn from the lessons of history.

Professor Tan Tai Yong: Well, that is the whole point of history, is it not? History is about changes over time; it happens in a certain context, its trajectory is never predetermined, and unexpected things happen.

And history is not about just reading standard texts, or accepting what you are told about the past. I think history loses its resonance if it is only learnt that way. History has to have personal meaning, and historical consciousness is a way of developing that.

History also tells us that decisions were made at a certain time in a certain context, with certain repercussions. It is easy to question past decisions with hindsight. But being able to appreciate the choices available to and challenges faced by previous generations — be it decision-makers, or one's immediate family, such as your father or mother — allows us to better understand their experiences.

If you looked at Singapore in the 1940s and 1950s, emerging out of colonialism and war, there were certain deprivations, challenges, political differences, and hopes. Decisions were taken and we went down a particular path. Will these be repeated, or is Singapore's future now predetermined? No, I think we will witness different challenges and contexts that may constrain the way we do things. So I would like to return to a recurring theme in my lectures — that there are continuities in our history, but history also moves off tangent at points in time. This uncertainty may not be comforting, but taking that broad view gives you a sense of where we have come from and where we might be headed.

Participant: My question has got to do with one very important building, which housed a very important family, for a very long time. As a historian, Professor Tan, what is your imagination about how this heritage should be preserved? Should we bulldoze it to the ground? Should we convert it to a garden of remembrance, or have the basement left standing? What role do the people have in contributing to the preservation of this historical building?

Prof. Tan: I will provide my personal view, that is to say, I am not speaking as a policymaker or representing the views of anyone but myself. If it were the last will and testament of Lee Kuan Yew to demolish his house — I assume that you are referring to his house at Oxley Road — then I think we should honour his wishes. Others will disagree and say that Lee is not an ordinary citizen and the house has national importance and historic value. My view is that there are many ways of remembering that. I do not think that we should preserve one part of the house, the basement or a garden, but maybe we can have a plaque there that says, here was the site at which the precursor of the PAP had its earliest meetings, and that would be historically sufficient.

I have seen houses in other parts of the world that are preserved to honour founding fathers and, sadly, they go into disrepair very quickly. After two generations, people forget the significance of these physical structures. And unless conservation is done carefully, 50 years down the road, these houses may just become one of those old museums that people do not care much about.

Participant: I would like to address the point that you raised about historical imagination. Could there be misplaced historical imagination? For instance, in our Primary Four Social Studies textbook, it is stated that Separation was a sad moment for the leaders and people in Singapore. Often, Separation is associated with the moment of anguish, when Mr Lee cried. But, in actual fact, on that day, in Chinatown, people were letting off firecrackers. There were some people who were excited. Of course, there were a number who were sad and anxious. But I think, sometimes, if the historical imagination is limited to a certain scene, such as that scene where Mr Lee cried, we end up over-generalising. We say that Separation was a sad day, when it was actually a day of mixed emotions.

Prof. Tan: I would not call it misplaced imagination. I think it is a question of how you interpret certain actions and events. History is complex. If you were to just zoom in on a particular point, you would only catch a glimpse of that one point. This reminds me of the analogy of the blind men and the elephant: if a man only feels one part of the elephant's body, he might say that the elephant is a wall; if another man feels its tail, he might say it is a rope. So, the question is how to zoom out and try to see something in its totality.

I do not think either reaction was wrong. Mr Lee, in 1965, was worried about what was going to happen to Singapore. He had planned to go into Malaysia and he had put his eggs in that basket, and then quite unexpectedly, after two years, Singapore was out. But of course there was the part of him that wanted to try and make Singapore work within Malaysia, notwithstanding the challenges. In this, he had the support of many members of his Cabinet. But, there were others in his team who were already disgruntled with the Merger and thinking of leaving Malaysia in 1964 because they felt that all the promises of a common market, of being able to get licenses to start industries in Singapore, were not coming to fruition. The situation was exacerbated by other tensions and conflict, such as the communal tensions and racial riots.

The leaders of the country were rightly concerned about what Singapore was going to be like after exiting Malaysia, amidst global and regional hostility. *Konfrontasi* was happening, as was the Cold War. So, from the point of view of Singapore's leaders, there were grounds for serious concern if Singapore left Malaysia. Maybe other people had different concerns and were happier to see Singapore out of Malaysia.

I would not say that there is misplaced historical imagination here; there were plainly different reactions to the same event.

Participant: You talked about how there is a need for people to engage with history, have historical consciousness. However, there seem to be certain limits to historical discourse in Singapore. I thought that it was quite interesting that you mentioned *The Art of Charlie Chan Hock Chye*, as it ran into some controversy and its grant from the National Arts Council was withdrawn, because its portrayals of players like Lim Chin Siong or Barisan Sosialis stepped on the toes of certain people. There seems to be a tension between historical imaginations and state interpretations of events. How does one deal with the limits to historical discourse within Singapore?

Prof. Tan: I have not personally encountered limits as a historian. I have written on Singapore history in the 1960s, spoken on themes of Singapore's evolution, lectured at National University of Singapore (NUS) and at Yale-NUS, and I do not think there have been limits placed on what I can or cannot say. But of course I have to be a responsible academic. Historical imagination is not about just saying anything you want and getting away with it. I think one has to be responsible in using evidence and explaining things in the right context. I brought up *The Art of Charlie Chan Hock Chye* as an example of historical imagination that stretches it as far as it could go, because Sonny Liew was able to move seamlessly between fact and fiction. However, he did not claim his work to be a history book and we should not take it as that. It is a graphic novel telling his story of Singapore.

Actually, there are two stories. One is the difficult life of a comic book writer, and the other is about how the context of Singapore has changed over time. Liew exercised his artistic license in his use of history. And if we can accept it for what it is, I do not think it is a case of looking at him as a kind of alternate historian who is trying to write a history that is not acceptable to Singapore. In my view, we do have space for different interpretations of Singapore history, to push the boundaries, appreciate nuance, and understand Singapore history in different ways, in order to learn and interpret our complex history.

Prof. Kwok: Sonny Liew also included in *The Art of Charlie Chan Hock Chye* a long bibliography referring to historical works.

Participant: An inference one can draw from Singapore's success is that it was successful because it was independent. How do you use that bit of history to suggest what its future should be?

Prof. Tan: I assume you mean independence from Malaysia. In my earlier lectures, I spoke about how Singapore has a past that preceded Malaysia.

Singapore has always been a port, even before the 20th century. In its more successful days, it has always been able to leverage its surrounding environment. For instance, it was able to plug into trade networks, and trade with the Chinese. It was able to operate within sultanates in the region. This dexterity accounted for Singapore's successes.

In 1965 after we exited from Malaysia, Singapore became a nation state. This placed certain constraints on how Singapore could do things. It had to function within the community of nations. But that did not and should not stop Singapore from having the independence to function as a global city-state and a port city.

When Singapore went into Malaysia in 1963, Malaysian Prime Minister Tunku Abdul Rahman had the idea that Singapore would be the New York of the Federation while Kuala Lumpur would be like Washington, D.C. Political control would reside in Kuala Lumpur, but Singapore could continue doing what it did to prosper and Malaysia would benefit. But there were other political problems. So I would say Singapore requires independence to function in ways that work for Singapore, and it has always treasured and developed this independence. It has exercised independence in its different forms as a colony, as a nation state, and as part of a federation.

Participant: My question is about the role of museums in preserving history. Singapore has built a number of very beautiful museums, designed to convey to the public the importance of history. However, the way that message is delivered — electronically, via computer screens — concerns me. This detracts from one very important function all museums are famous for, which is the preservation of artefacts.

Prof. Tan: Museums are very difficult to run these days because the demography is so diverse. I agree that you must be able to show and use artefacts to tell the story, and based on my involvement with museums in Singapore, I know that no effort or expense has been spared to purchase valuable artefacts that can enrich and make public exhibitions more compelling.

But sometimes, young people do not want to see old objects only. They want to feel and touch and get an interactive experience. So museums now have to find ways to cater to different audiences, displaying authentic artefacts for the general public, but at the same time using technology to engage young people. It is always a combination of both.

Participant: We often use the term "on the wrong side of history." What are some of the global trends you think Singapore might be in danger of being on the wrong side of history? For example, the rise of China and our relations with China, LGBTQ rights, Singapore vis-à-vis the rest of Southeast Asia. There is a global trend, but Singapore has often embraced our difference.

Prof. Tan: There seems to be an underlying assumption here that one knows how history is going to evolve, and therefore you can place yourself on the right or wrong side of history. However, it is hard to say whether we are on the right or wrong side of history without adequate information, and without understanding the constraints that our decision-makers may have to work with, which is why I have discussed the importance of context. You make a decision based on what you believe is important, with all the limitations that you have to work with, in the context that is relevant to you now. You may observe that the global trend seems to be greater liberalisation with certain attitudinal changes, but not everybody would see things the same way. If you have to make a decision, you would have to balance opposing stances and you may seek a *modus vivendi* that pleases as many people as possible, but that is not always easy.

I guess the important thing in this regard is not history, but foresight. In other words, if you were to look ahead five or 10 years, what would the scenario be like? You could make a judgement call, it turns out to be wrong, and then on hindsight, you are said to be on the wrong side of history. Or you may be right and then people will say, "Wow, you are really ahead of your time, you could read the situation very well." So, as a historian, I will make that judgment 50 years down the road, if you would still hear me then, and I will tell you whether Singapore's current policies are on the right or wrong side of history!

But we are responding and adapting, and I think Singapore is especially good at that because its small size allows it to move very quickly. I was once told by a minister that changing educational policy in a big country is a massive task because there are so many layers of governance — federal, state, district, etc. In contrast, in Singapore, he could call all the principals to sit in a room, so that they all hear from him directly on the policy decisions. So, size does help in Singapore's case, and there is a lot of anticipation and planning for what might happen. At the same time, we should not forget to look at the past, because it offers us interesting lessons that we can draw on.

Participant: As far as conservation and demolition in Singapore is concerned, policymakers know that we are going to be on the wrong side of history, and yet, they are not doing anything about it. Architecture built from the 1940s to 1970s has been demolished, and we still continue to demolish buildings, while replacing them with worse things. Why is this sense of history not communicated to policymakers who are making the wrong decisions? Our younger generation often cannot make these demands or requests — they do not know what used to exist because most of those buildings are already gone. It is not just schools and neighbourhoods. Today, we knowingly demolish many of our buildings that were built post-independence. In future, new governments will have nothing to say because everything would have been gone.

Prof. Tan: If I were not involved with the National Heritage Board in any way, and speaking as a total outsider, I might have similar views. But having been involved in some ways, I can see that there have been efforts to try to understand and preserve Singapore's heritage, and moves are being made to study the viability of conservation.

But there are always tradeoffs. In fairness to the government, I would say that they are trying their best but sometimes when you adopt a policy, people are going to be affected, possibly unhappy, and you have to accept that. I do not think it is the case that nothing is being done, or that the government is totally oblivious, or does not care. But perhaps more can be done.

Participant: I am a history graduate and museum docent, and I have two points to make. My first point has to do with museums. Prof Tan flashed the picture of the knee-jerk reaction to the renaming of the Syonan Gallery. I am a guide there and, unfortunately, visitors often think that it is nothing but a museum of automobiles. Maybe retaining the old name, "Memories at Old Ford Factory", would have been better than calling it the Former Ford Factory.

My second point is, as a history graduate, I have peers who have been labelled as revisionist historians. Although you say you welcome the revising of history, many of our archival materials are still not open. Our archives have not been opened to allow us, for example, to judge if the Marxist conspiracy was right or wrong, and if there are people who should have been exonerated, rather than still being labelled as subversives.

Prof. Tan: I am, of course, not speaking for the government here, but as a historian. Revisionist history has been used to describe people who write a certain form of history that does not tally with an official narration. I do not think revisionism is bad or wrong because I think all historians, in fact, all academics, revise scholarship. Using new evidence and new interpretations, we try to push the boundaries of knowledge. In the process, we revise the narrative — this is revisionism in scholarship.

I fully agree that, for more people to do historical research, materials have to be available. Perhaps National Archives should declassify more consistently and regularly, so that historians can go in and have a look at materials, and then interpret particular events using new evidence. Maybe this will happen gradually, and the National Archives and National Library Board will try to see whether they can make more material available as Singapore progresses.

Our National Library Board Act says that public records of national or historical significance which are more than 25 years old "shall be transferred to the care and control of the National Archives."[1] But there is a whole host of reasons why records have not been made public. One reason is that, as organisations grow, evolve, and move, some records are lost because they have not been properly stored and archived. I think Singapore does not have an archiving culture. Maybe this will change and we will have access to better records and, on the basis of those records, develop a better understanding of our history.

Prof. Kwok: Tai Yong, I would like to push that point a little more, because we spoke about painful and traumatic memories, and in your previous dialogue with Professor Wang Gungwu, he mentioned history being written from the viewpoint of the victors. There are not only the losers; some might see themselves as victims, too. At times, the very subject of history, or particular episodes, may seem to be almost taboo and unspeakable. Things may change as time goes along. But in the meantime, there could be some people who still feel a sense of woundedness, and struggle to find some voice to place on record their version. What would you say to that?

Prof. Tan: I say, all power to them — they should write their versions. I do not think anybody should be stopped from telling their own story. We should listen to a range of stories, because that will enrich our understanding. Listening to just a single version, interpretation, or narrative will narrow and limit our worldview. I have in my library many books written by people who were "defeated" in the 1960s. I find their stories compelling. I do not always agree with their interpretation of the events, but reading their personal accounts certainly enriches my understanding

---

[1] Attorney-General's Chambers, "National Library Board Act," Singapore Statutes Online, accessed 31 August 2019, https://sso.agc.gov.sg/Act/NLBA1995.

of what happened. That to me is historical consciousness — to have a feel of that time and place, to learn how people acted, to try and understand the thinking and motivations of those people. I think it is time we move beyond the dichotomy between them and us, to instead see the different individuals as a group of people all trying to envision a future for Singapore. They may have had different views and visions, but they were all nationalists, trying to find answers as Singapore emerged from colonial rule. When you see that, then you avoid holding a simplistic view of victors versus the vanquished, heroes versus villains, and winners versus losers. You see them as a group of Singaporeans trying to articulate their respective visions for their country.

Prof. Kwok: What we have witnessed, not just tonight, but in this entire series, is the mind of a historian thinking aloud and sharing with us what it means to have historical consciousness and historical imagination. Tai Yong, it turns out that you are a pretty good storyteller, too. I would just like to close with a small point that might be fleshed out down the road: the idea that the study of history and historical reflection are perhaps linked not just to critical judgment, but also moral reasoning — about what could have been, what should have been, and maybe what would have been. These outcomes did not pan out for many reasons, which we can now try to understand, but they also extend, widen and deepen our imagination.

Prof. Tan: I will answer with one word: empathy. I think we need to have empathy about what happened in the past so that we can better understand others and ourselves. If you only use the past to judge, you will always have to take sides. But if you are prepared to empathise and embrace various interpretations, I think you will be able to have a more inclusive, nuanced sense of the past that has shaped all of us in different ways.

Bibliography

Amrith, Sunil S. *Crossing the Bay of Bengal.* Cambridge, Massachusetts, and London, England: Harvard University Press, 2013.

Amrith, Sunil S. *Migration and Diaspora in Modern Asia.* New York: Cambridge University Press, 2011.

Anderson, Benedict. *Imagined Communities.* London and New York: Verso, 1991.

Ang, Ien, and Jon Stratton. "The Singapore Way of Multiculturalism: Western Concepts/Asian Cultures." *Sojourn* 10, no. 1 (April 1995): 65–89.

Anuar, Mazelan. "Early Malay Printing in Singapore." *BiblioAsia* 13, Issue 3, October 17, 2017. http://www.nlb.gov.sg/biblioasia/2017/10/07/early-malay-printing-in-singapore/

Attorney-General's Chambers. "Constitution of the Republic of Singapore Part XIII — General Provisions — Article 152: Minorities and Special Position of Malays." Singapore Statutes Online, accessed 17 June 2019. https://sso.agc.gov.sg/Act/CONS1963?ValidDate=20170401&ProvIds=P1XIII-.

Attorney-General's Chambers. "National Library Board Act." Singapore Statutes Online, accessed 31 August 2019. https://sso.agc.gov.sg/Act/NLBA1995.

Ballantyne, Tony. *Orientalism and Race: Aryanism in the British Empire.* Basingstoke: Palgrave Macmillan, 2006.

Ballantyne, Tony. *Webs of Empire: Locating New Zealand's Colonial Past.* Vancouver: UBC Press, The University of British Columbia, 2014.

Basu, Dilip K. *The Rise and Growth of the Colonial Port Cities in Asia.* Berkeley: University Press of America, 1985.

Bhaskaran, Manu. "An Architect of the Singapore Miracle." *The Business Times* (Singapore). March 25, 2015. https://www.businesstimes.com.sg/government-economy/lee-kuan-yew-dies/an-architect-of-the-singapore-miracle.

Birch, Ernest W. "The Vernacular Press in the Straits." *Journal of the Straits Branch of the Royal Asiatic Society* 4 (December, 1879): 51–55.

Bird, James Harold. *Seaports and Seaport Terminals*. London: Hutchinson & Co, 1971.

Blackburn, Kevin. "Mary Turnbull's History Textbook for the Singapore Nation," in *Studying Singapore's Past: C.M. Turnbull and the History of Modern Singapore*, edited by Nicholas Tarling, 65–86. Singapore: NUS Press, 2012.

Bogaars, George. "The Effect of the Opening of the Suez Canal on the Trade and Development of Singapore." *Journal of the Malayan Branch of the Royal Asiatic Society* 28, no. 1 (169) (1955): 208–51.

Borschberg, Peter. "Singapore in the Cycles of the Longue Durée," *Journal of the Malaysian Branch of the Royal Asiatic Society* 90, no.1, June 2017: 30–60.

Burdett, Ricky, and Sudjic, Deyan. *The Endless City*. London: Phaidon Press, 2007.

Carey, Hilary M. *Empires of Religion*. Basingstoke: Palgrave Macmillan, 2008.

Carr, E.H. *What is History?* London: Penguin Books, [1961] 2018.

Chakrabarty, Dipesh. "Minority Histories, Subaltern Pasts." *Economic and Political Weekly* 33 no. 9 (February 28, 1998): 473–79.

Chang, David W. "Nation-Building in Singapore." *Asian Survey* 8, no. 9 (1968): 761–73. https://doi.org/10.2307/2642643.

Chua, Beng Huat. "Racial Singaporeans: Absence after the Hyphen." In *Southeast Asian Identities: Culture and the Politics of Representation in Indonesia, Malaysia, Singapore, and Thailand*, edited by Joel S. Kahn, 28–50. Singapore: Institute of Southeast Asian Studies, 1998.

Churchill, Winston. "First Speech as Prime Minister to House of Commons (Blood, Toil, Tears and Sweat)." The International Churchill Society. May 13, 1940. https://winstonchurchill.org/resources/speeches/1940-the-finest-hour/blood-toil-tears-and-sweat-2/.

Coclanis, Peter. *Time's Arrow, Time's Cycle: Globalisation in Southeast Asia Over La Longue Durée*. Singapore: Institute of Southeast Asian Studies, 2006.

Constitutional Talks in London, *Singapore Legislative Assembly Debates*, 1st ser., vol. 3 (5 March 1957), col. 1457.

Curtis, Simon. *Global Cities and Global Order*. Oxford and New York: Oxford University Press, 2016.

Devan, Janadas. "Opening Remarks at Institute of Policy Studies Annual Flagship Conference Singapore Perspectives 2018." Singapore Perspectives conference. January 22, 2018. https://lkyspp.nus.edu.sg/docs/default-source/ips/singapore-perspectives-2018_opening-remarks_final799d057b46bc6210a3aaff0100138661.pdf.

Devan, Janadas. "Exceptional Government to Sustain a Nation Once Thought Improbable." IPS Commons. January 23, 2017, https://www.ipscommons.sg/exceptional-government-to-sustain-a-nation-once-thought-improbable/.

Duiker, William J. *The Rise of Nationalism in Vietnam: 1900–1941*. Ithaca and London: Cornell University Press, 1976.

Enterprise Singapore. "Malaysia: Market Profile." Last updated on February 26, 2019. https://www.enterprisesg.gov.sg/overseas-markets/asia-pacific/Malaysia/market-profile.

Evers, Hans-Dieter, and Pavadarayan, Jayarani. *Asceticism and Ecstasy: The Chettiars of Singapore*. Bielefeld: Forschungsschwerpunkt Entwicklungssoziologie, Fakultat fur Soziologie, Universitat Bielefeld, 1980.

Fifield, Russell H. "Southeast Asia as a Regional Concept." *Southeast Asian Journal of Social Science* 11, no. 2 (1983): 1–14.

Freedman, Jonathan. "'The Ethics of Identity': A Rooted Cosmopolitan." *The New York Times*, June 12, 2005, https://www.nytimes.com/2005/06/12/books/review/the-ethics-of-identity-a-rooted-cosmopolitan.html.

Frost, Mark R., and Balasingamchow, Yu-Mei. *Singapore: A Biography.* Singapore: Editions Didier Millet and National Museum of Singapore, 2012.

Frost, Mark. "'Wider Opportunities': Religious Revival, Nationalist Awakening and the Global Dimension in Colombo, 1870–1920." *Modern Asian Studies* 36, no. 4 (October 2002): 937–967, https://doi.org/10.1017/S0026749X02004067.

Greenway, Hugh D. S. "Interview with Prime Minister Mr. Lee Kuan Yew." National Archives Online. June 10, 1969. http://www.nas.gov.sg/archivesonline/data/pdfdoc/lky19690610.pdf.

Ghosh, Amitav. *River of Smoke.* New York: Farrar, Straus and Giroux, 2011.

Government of Singapore. "Do You Know How Many Types of Foreign Workers We Have in Singapore?" Factually (Ministry of Communications and Information website). March 2013, http://www.gov.sg/factually/content/do-you-know-how-many-types-of-foreign-workers-we-have-in-singapore.

Hack, Karl. "Framing Singapore's History." In *Studying Singapore's Past: C. M. Turnbull and the History of Modern Singapore*, edited by Nicholas Tarling, 17–64. Singapore: NUS Press, 2012.

Harari, Yuval Noah. *Homo Deus: A Brief History of Tomorrow.* London: Vintage, 2016.

Harper, T.N. "Globalism and the Pursuit of Authenticity: The Making of a Diasporic Public Sphere in Singapore." *Sojourn* 12, no. 2 (1997): 261–92.

Harper, T.N. "Lim Chin Siong and the 'Singapore Story,'" In *Comet In Our Sky: Lim Chin Siong In History*, edited by Tan Jing Quee and Jomo K. S., 3–55. Kuala Lumpur: INSAN, 2001.

Hein, Carola. *Port Cities: Dynamic Landscapes and Global Networks*. London and New York: Routledge, 2011.

Heng, Geraldine. Preface to "Whose Middle Ages?" (unpublished manuscript).

Heng, Swee Keat, "2019 Budget Statement," Ministry of Finance Singapore, February 18, 2019, https://www.singaporebudget.gov.sg/budget_2019/budget-speech.

Hill Michael, and Lian, Kwen Fee. *The Politics of Nation Building and Citizenship in Singapore* (London: Routledge, 1995).

Ho, Engseng. "Inter-Asian Concepts for Mobile Societies." *The Journal of Asian Studies* 76, no. 4 (November 2017): 907–28.

Hopkins, Anthony G. "Introduction: Globalization — An Agenda for Historians." In *Globalization in World History*. London: Pimlico, 2002.

Hong, Lysa, and Huang Jianli. *The Scripting of a National History: Singapore and its Pasts*. Singapore: NUS Press, 2008.

Hong Kong Marine Department. "Ranking of Container Ports of the World." April 2018. https://www.mardep.gov.hk/en/publication/pdf/portstat_2_y_b5.pdf.

Huang, Jianli. "Bicentennial Commemoration of Raffles' Landing in Singapore: Preparatory Steps and History Dilemmas." *Yihe Shiji* (Ee Hoe Hean Club publication), no. 36 (July 2018): 8–19.

Huff, W. G. *The Economic Growth of Singapore: Trade and Development in the Twentieth Century*. Cambridge: Cambridge University Press, 1994. https://doi.org/10.1017/CBO9780511470714.

Jakobsen, Erik W., Mellbye, Christian Svane, Osman, M. Shahrin, and Dyrstad, Eirik H. "The Leading Maritime Capitals of the World 2017." Menon Economics, 2017.

Kementerian Kewangan Malaysia. "Malaysia's Trade with Major Trading Partners." 2017. http://www.treasury.gov.my/pdf/economy/er/1617/st3_1.pdf.

Kidwai, Atiya Habeeb. "Conceptual and Methodological Issues: Ports, Port Cities and Port-Hinterlands." In *Ports and Their Hinterlands in India, 1700–1950*, edited by Indu Banga, 7–43. New Delhi: Manohar Publications, 1992.

Kim, Hin Ho David, and Ho, Mun Wai. *Singapore Chronicles: Gateways*. Singapore: Straits Times Press, 2016.

Kissinger, Henry. *World Order*. New York: Penguin Press, 2014.

Koh, Gillian, Soon, Debbie, and Leong, Chan-Hoong. "IPS Survey on Emigration Attitudes of Young Singaporeans (2016)." Institute of Policy Studies. September 28, 2018, https://lkyspp.nus.edu.sg/ips/news/details/ips-survey-on-emigration-attitudes-of-young-singaporeans-2016?fbrefresh=636957795396131050.

Kwa, Chong Guan. "From Temasek to Singapore: Locating a Global City-State in the Cycles of Melaka Straits History." In *Early Singapore: 1300s–1819*, edited by John Miksic and Cheryl-Ann Low Mei Gek. Singapore: Singapore History Museum, 2004, 124–146.

Kwa, Chong Guan, and S Rajaratnam. "PAP's First Ten Years." In *S Rajaratnam on Singapore: From Ideas to Reality*. Singapore: World Scientific, 2006, 180–226.

Kwa, Chong Guan. *Pre-Colonial Singapore*. Singapore: Institute of Policy Studies, National University of Singapore and Straits Times Press, 2017.

Kwa, Chong Guan, Derek Heng, and Tan Tai Yong, *Singapore: A 700 Year History*. Singapore: National Archives of Singapore, 2009.

Lai, Chee Kien. "Multi-Ethnic Enclaves Around Middle Road: An Examination of Early Urban Settlement in Singapore." *BiblioAsia* 2, Issue 12, July 2006.

Lau, Albert. "Nation-Building and the Singapore Story: Some Issues in the Study of Contemporary Singapore History." In *Nation-Building: Five Southeast Asian Histories*, edited by Wang Gungwu, 221–50. Singapore: Institute of Southeast Asian Studies, 2005.

Lee, Hsien Loong. "Speech by BG (NS) Lee Hsien Loong, Deputy Prime Minister, at the Launch of National Education at Television Corporation of Singapore (TCS) TV Theatre on Friday, 17 May 1997 at 9.30am." National Archives of Singapore, http://www.nas.gov.sg/archivesonline/speeches/record-details/77e6b874-115d-11e3-83d5-0050568939ad.

Lee, Kuan Yew. "How Will Singapore Compete in a Global Economy (Speech by Senior Minister Lee Kuan Yew to Nanyang Technological University (NTU)/National University of Singapore (NUS) Students, Tue 15 Feb 2000)." Ministry of Information and The Arts, February 15, 2000. http://www.nas.gov.sg/archivesonline/speeches/view-html?filename=2000021502.htm.

Lee, Kuan Yew, *From Third World to First — The Singapore Story: 1965–2000*, 2nd edition. Singapore: Marshall Cavendish Editions and Straits Times Press, 2014.

Lee, Kuan Yew. "Speech by Prime Minister Lee Kuan Yew at His 60th Birthday." September 16, 1983. http://www.nas.gov.sg/archivesonline/speeches/record-details/73f6398a-115d-11e3-83d5-0050568939ad.

Lee, Kuan Yew. *The Singapore Story: Memoirs of Lee Kuan Yew*. Singapore: Times Edition, 1998.

Lee, Kuan Yew. "Transcript of Speech by the Prime Minister, Mr Lee Kuan Yew, at the Reunion Dinner of St. Andrew's Old Boys' Association on 7th September, 1968." September 7, 1968, http://www.nas.gov.sg/archivesonline/data/pdfdoc/lky19680907.pdf.

Lee, Kuan Yew. "Transcript of a Speech in English by the Prime Minister at a Luncheon Given by the Pasir Panjang Residents at Perak House on 5th December, 1965." December 5, 1965, http://www.nas.gov.sg/archivesonline/data/pdfdoc/lky19651205b.pdf.

Lee, Kuan Yew. "Will Malaysia Succeed? (Speech of the Prime Minister at the Luncheon of the Singapore National Union of Journalists on Friday, 24th May, 1963)." Ministry of Culture, May 24, 1963. http://www.nas.gov.sg/archivesonline/speeches/record-details/73dc7cdc-115d-11e3-83d5-0050568939ad.

Lee, Meiyu. "A Dictionary that Bridged Two Races." *BiblioAsia* 11, Issue 4, January 26, 2016, http://www.nlb.gov.sg/biblioasia/2016/01/26/a-dictionary-that-bridged-two-races/#sthash.pNEVuwEl.dpbs.

Lee, Soo Ann. *Singapore: From Place to Nation*, 4th edition. Singapore: Pearson Education, 2019.

Levi, Primo. *The Drowned and the Saved*. London: Abacus, 1989.

Lewis, Su Lin. *Cities in Motion: Urban Life and Cosmopolitanism in Southeast Asia, 1920–1940*. Cambridge: Cambridge University Press, 2016.

Lim, Lydia. "Identity in Singapore Version 4.0." In *Commentary 27 (2018) SGP 4.0: An Agenda*, edited by Gillian Koh, 95–99. Singapore: the National University of Singapore Society (NUSS). http://www.nuss.org.sg/publication/1548232969_commentary2018_Vol27_FINAL.pdf.

Loh, Wei Leng, and Seow, Jeffrey. *Through Turbulent Terrain: Trade of the Straits Port of Penang*. Kuala Lumpur: Malaysian Branch of the Royal Asiatic Society, 2018.

Luce, Edward. "US Declining Interest in History Presents Risk to Democracy." *Financial Times*, May 2, 2019. https://www.ft.com/content/e19d957c-6ca3-11e9-80c7-60ee53e6681d.

Markovits, Claude. "Ethnicity, Locality and Circulation in Two Diasporic Merchant Networks from South Asia." In *The South Asian Diaspora: Transnational Networks and Changing Identities*, edited by Rajesh Rai and Peter Reeves, 28–44. Abingdon, Oxon: Routledge, 2009.

Maslan, Aiza. "Hajj and the Malayan Experience, 1860s–1941." *Kemanusiaan* 21, no. 2 (2014): 79–98.

Mathews, Mathew, Lim, Leonard, Shanthini S., and Cheung, Nicole. "CNA-IPS Survey on Ethnic Identity in Singapore." *IPS Working Papers No. 28*, November 2017.

Mazelan, Anuar. "Early Malay Printing in Singapore." *BiblioAsia*, 13, Issue 3, October 7, 2017. http://www.nlb.gov.sg/biblioasia/2017/10/07/early-malay-printing-in-singapore/.

McPherson, Kenneth. *The Indian Ocean: A History of People and the Sea.* Delhi: Oxford University Press, 1993.

Miksic, John, and Low, Mei Gek Cheryl-Ann. *Early Singapore, 1300s–1819: Evidence in Maps, Text and Artefacts.* Singapore: Singapore History Museum, 2004.

Miller, Michael B. "Pilgrims' Progress: The Business of the Hajj." *Past & Present* 191, no. 1 (2006): 189–228.

Ministry of Information and the Arts. "PM Goh Chok Tong's National Day Rally 2001 Speech, 19 Aug 2001." National Archives of Singapore, August 19, 2001. http://www.nas.gov.sg/archivesonline/speeches/view-html?filename=2001081903.htm.

Ministry of Information, Communications and the Arts. "Speech by Mr Lee Hsien Loong, Prime Minister and Minister for Finance, at the Opening of Global Entrepolis @ Singapore 2004." National Archives of Singapore, October 11, 2004, http://www.nas.gov.sg/archivesonline/speeches/view-html?filename=2004101192.htm.

Mukund, Kanakalatha. "Trade and Merchants: The Vijayanagar Period (1400–1600)." In *The Trading World of the Tamil Merchant: Evolution of Merchant Capitalism in the Coromandel*, 42–52. Hyderabad: Orient Longman, 1999.

Murphey, Rhoads. "On the Evolution of the Port City." In *Brides of the Sea: Port Cities of Asia From the 16th to the 20th Centuries*, edited by Frank Broeze, 223–245. Honolulu: University of Hawaii Press, 1989.

National Archives of Singapore. "Connecting Singapore To The World — From Submarine Cables to Satellite Earth Stations." Policy History @ ArchivesOnline, June 24, 2016. http://www.nas.gov.sg/archivesonline/policy_history/connecting-singapore-to-the-world.

National Archives, United Kingdom. "Relations Between Federation of Malaya and Singapore, 1960–1961." Colonial Office and Commonwealth Office: Far Eastern Department and successors: Registered Files (FED Series). CO 1030/973: File no. FED 59/03/01 Part B.

National Archives, United Kingdom. "Relations Between Federation of Malaya and Singapore, 1959–1960." Colonial Office and Commonwealth Office: Far Eastern Department and successors: Registered Files (FED Series). CO 1030/972: File no. FED 59/03/01 Part A.

National Library Board Singapore. "Singapore is Conferred City Status — Singapore History, 22nd Sep 1951." HistorySG, 2014. http://eresources.nlb.gov.sg/history/events/7333873b-d517-4a75-b828-331a30673b30#1.

Nik Hassan, Nik Ahmad Bin Haji. "The Malay Press." *Journal of the Malayan Branch of the Royal Asiatic Society* 36, no. 1 (201) (May 1963): 37–78.

Nye, Joseph. "Globalism Versus Globalization." *The Globalist*, April 15, 2002. https://www.theglobalist.com/globalism-versus-globalization/.

Olds, Kris, and Yeung, Henry. "Pathways to Global City Formation: A View from the Developmental City-State of Singapore." *Review of International Political Economy* 11, no. 3 (June 1, 2004): 489–521. https://doi.org/10.1080/0969229042000252873.

Ooi, Kee Beng. "Southeast Asia and Foreign Empires." In *The Eurasian Core and Its Edges: Dialogues with Wang Gungwu on the History of the World*, 94–140. Singapore: Institute of Southeast Asian Studies, 2014.

Pang, Alvin. "City of a Thousand Histories; Island of a Thousand Cities." In *The Birthday Book: What Should We Never Forget*, edited by Sheila Pakir and Malminderjit Singh, 1–10. Singapore: Ethos Books, 2017.

Paul, Anju Mary. *Local Encounters in a Global City: Singapore Stories.* Singapore: Ethos Books, 2017.

Peacock, James L. "Plural Society in Southeast Asia." *The High School Journal* 56, no. 1 (1972): 56–68.

Peleggi, Maurizio. "The Social and Material Life of Colonial Hotels: Comfort Zones as Contact Zones in British Colombo and Singapore, ca. 1870–1930." *Journal of Social History* 46, no. 1 (2012): 124–53.

Perry, John Curtis. *Singapore: Unlikely Power.* New York: Oxford University Press, 2017.

Pruessen, Ronald W., Tan, Tai Yong, and Frey, Marc. *The Transformation of Southeast Asia: International Perspectives on Decolonization.* Singapore: NUS Press, 2003.

Quah, Jon S. T. "Globalization and Singapore's Search for Nationhood." In *Nationalism and Globalization: East and West*, edited by Leo Suryadinata, 71–101. Singapore: Institute of Southeast Asian Studies, 2000.

Rajaratnam, S. "Singapore: Global City." In *S Rajaratnam on Singapore: From Ideas to Reality*, edited by Kwa Chong Guan, 227–37. Singapore: World Scientific, 2006.

Rajaratnam, S. "Speech by Mr S Rajaratnam, Second Deputy Prime Minister (Foreign Affairs), at a seminar on 'Adaptive Reuse: Integrating Traditional Areas into the Modern Urban Fabric' held at the Shangri-La Hotel, April 28, 1984 at 10.30am." National Archives of Singapore, http://www.nas.gov.sg/archivesonline/speeches/record-details/79c7d80b-115d-11e3-83d5-0050568939ad.

Rajaratnam, S. "Speech by S Rajaratnam, Senior Minister (Prime Minister's Office) at the official opening of the exhibition 'A Vision of the Past' at the National Museum Art Gallery on Thursday, 14 May 1987 at 6.10pm." National Archives of Singapore. http://www.nas.gov.sg/archivesonline/ speeches/record-details/723c23ee-115d-11e3-83d5-0050568939ad.

Rajaratnam, S. "Text of Address Titled 'Singapore: Global City', by Mr S Rajaratnam, Minister for Foreign Affairs, to the Singapore Press Club on February 6, 1972." National Archives of Singapore. http://www.nas. gov.sg/archivesonline/data/pdfdoc/PressR19720206a.pdf.

Ray, Rajat Kanta. "Asian Capital in the Age of European Domination: The Rise of the Bazaar, 1800–1914." *Modern Asian Studies* 29, no. 3 (July, 1995): 495–554.

Reeves, Peter, Broeze, Frank, and McPherson, Kenneth. "Studying the Asian Port City." In *Brides of the Sea: Port Cities of Asia From the 16th to the 20th Centuries*, edited by Frank Broeze, 29–53. Honolulu: University of Hawaii Press, 1989.

Reid, Anthony. "Cosmopolis and Nation in Central Southeast Asia," Asia Research Institute Working Paper Series, April 22, 2004.

Reid, Anthony. "Economic and Social Change, c.1400–1800." In *The Cambridge History of Southeast Asia: Vol. 1, From Early Times to c. 1800, part 2*, edited by Nicholas Tarling, 460–507. Cambridge: Cambridge University Press, 1992.

Reid, Anthony. *Southeast Asia in the Age of Commerce, 1450–1680*. (New Haven: Yale University Press, 1990).

Report of the Commission appointed by the Governor of Hong Kong to enquire into the causes and effects of the present trade depression in Hong Kong and make recommendations for the amelioration of the existing position and for the improvement of the trade of the Colony (1935) Hong Kong. Hong Kong: Noronha & Co., 1935. https://catalogue.nla.gov.au/Record/2939499.

Riddell, Peter G. "Arab Migrants and Islamization in the Malay World During the Colonial Period." *Indonesia and the Malay World* 29, no. 84 (2001): 113–28.

Roff, William R. "The Malayo-Muslim World of Singapore at the Close of the Nineteenth Century." *The Journal of Asian Studies* 24, no. 1 (1964): 75–90.

Sandhu, K. S., and Mani, A. *Indian Communities in Southeast Asia*. Singapore: Institute of Southeast Asian Studies, 1993.

Schrader, Heiko. "Chettiar Finance in Colonial Asia." *Zeitschrift Für Ethnologie* 121, no. 1 (1996): 101–26.

Shome, Raka. "Mapping the Limits of Multiculturalism in the Context of Globalization," *International Journal of Communication* 6 (2012): 144–65.

Siddique, Sharon. *Asian Port Cities: Uniting Land and Water Worlds*. Singapore: Lee Kuan Yew Centre for Innovative Cities, 2016.

Sim, Fann. "Going Beyond 1819: How Well do Singaporeans Know the History of Singapore?" *Channel NewsAsia*, February 17, 2018. https://www.channelnewsasia.com/news/singapore/going-beyond-1819-how-well-do-singaporeans-know-the-history-of-9945420.

"Singapore's Bicentennial Commemoration in 2019: A Time to Reflect on its Rich History." *Channel NewsAsia*, 31 December 2017. https://www.channelnewsasia.com/news/singapore/singapore-s-bicentennial-commemoration-in-2019-a-time-to-reflect-9823248.

Singapore Department of Statistics. "Singapore International Trade." Statistics Singapore — Singapore International Trade, 2019, http://www.singstat.gov.sg/modules/infographics/singapore-international-trade.

Sopiee, Mohamed Noordin. *From Malayan Union to Singapore Separation: Political Unification in the Malaysia Region, 1945–65*. Kuala Lumpur: Penerbit Universiti Malaya, 1974.

Southgate, Beverley C. *History: What and Why? Ancient, Modern, and Postmodern Perspectives*. London, New York: Routledge, 1996.

Suppiah, Ummadevi, and Raja, Sivachandralingam Sundara. *The Chettiar Role in Malaysia's Economic History*. Kuala Lumpur, Malaysia: University of Malaya Press, 2016.

Tan, Tai Yong. *Creating "Greater Malaysia": Decolonization and the Politics of Merger*. Singapore: Institute of Southeast Asian Studies, 2008.

Tan, Tai Yong. "Port Cities and Hinterlands: A Comparative Study of Singapore and Calcutta." *Political Geography* 26, no. 7 (September 2007): 851–65.

Tan, Tai Yong. "Singapore's Story: A Port City in Search of Hinterlands." In *Port Cities in Asia and Europe*, edited by Arndt Graf and Chua Beng Huat. Abingdon, Oxon: Taylor and Francis, 2009. https://doi.org/10.4324/9780203884515-21.

Tarling, Nicholas. *Nations and States in Southeast Asia*. Cambridge: Cambridge University Press, 1998.

Teng, Angela. "The Big Read: The Foreigner Issue — Are We Ready for a Rethink?" *TODAYonline*, February 3, 2018. https://www.todayonline.com/singapore/big-read-foreigner-issue-are-we-ready-rethink.

Turnbull, Constance Mary. *A History of Singapore, 1819–1988*, 2nd edition. Singapore: Oxford University Press, 1989.

Wang, Gungwu. *The Nanhai Trade: The Early History of Chinese Trade in the South China Sea*. Singapore: Times Academic Press, 1998.

Wang, Gungwu. *Renewal: The Chinese State and the New Global History*. Hong Kong: Chinese University Press, 2013.

Warren, James Francis. *Ah Ku and Karayuki-san: Prostitution in Singapore 1870–1940*. Singapore: Oxford University Press, 1993.

Warren, James Francis. *Rickshaw Coolie: A People's History of Singapore, 1880–1940*. Singapore: NUS Press, [1986] 2003.

Wong, Lin Ken. "Singapore: Its Growth as an Entrepot Port, 1819-1941." *Journal of Southeast Asian Studies* 9, no. 1 (1978): 50–84.

Wong, Lin Ken. "The Trade of Singapore, 1819-69." *Journal of the Malayan Branch of the Royal Asiatic Society* 33, no. 4 (192) (1960): 4–315.

Wong, Lin Ken. "Commercial Growth Before the Second World War." In *A History of Singapore*, edited by Ernest C.T. Chew and Edwin Lee, 48–52. Singapore: Oxford University Press, 1991.

Yahaya, Nurfadzilah. "Alternate Pasts: Politics of Commemoration of 1915," presented at "The Future of Our Pasts" festival, Singapore, February 27, 2019.

Yahaya, Nurfadzilah. "Good Friends and Dangerous Enemies — British Images of the Arab Elite in Colonial Singapore (1819–1942)." Master's dissertation, Department of History, National University of Singapore, 2006.

Yap, Yan Hong. Oral History Interview (Singapore, 1989), National Archives of Singapore.

Yeo, George. *George Yeo on Bonsai, Banyan and the Tao*, edited by Asad-ul Iqbal Latif and Lee Huay Leng. Singapore: World Scientific, 2015.

Yeo, George. "Overcoming the Vulnerabilities of a Small Nation (Speech at the Temasek Seminar on 7 November '96)." Ministry of Information & The Arts, November 7, 1996. http://www.nas.gov.sg/archivesonline/speeches/view-html?filename=1996110607.htm.

Yeo, George. "Speech on Information Technology and Singapore's Future." Keynote address at EMASIA, Los Angeles, June 4, 1998. National Archives of Singapore. http://www.nas.gov.sg/archivesonline/speeches/view-html?filename=1998060502.htm

Yeoh, Brenda S. A. "Changing Conceptions of Space in History Writing: A Selective Mapping of Writings on Singapore." In *At the Interstices and on the Margins: New Terrains in Southeast Asian History*, edited by Abu Talib Ahmad and Tan Liok Ee, 30–55. Athens: Ohio University Press, 2003.

Yeoh, Brenda S. A. "Cosmopolitanism and Its Exclusions in Singapore." In *Globalisation and the Politics of Forgetting*, edited by Yong-Sook Lee and Brenda S. A. Yeoh, 137–52. London: Routledge, 2006.

Yeoh, Brenda S. A., and Chang T. C. "Globalising Singapore: Debating Transnational Flows in the City." *Urban Studies* 38, no. 7 (2001): 1028, https://doi.org/10.1080/00420980123947.

Yeoh, Brenda, and Lin, Weiqiang. "Rapid Growth in Singapore's Immigrant Population Brings Policy Challenges." Migration Policy Institute, April 3, 2012, https://www.migrationpolicy.org/article/rapid-growth-singapores-immigrant-population-brings-policy-challenges.

Zaccheus, Melody. "The Balance Between National Progress and Preservation of Heritage." *The Straits Times*, May 6, 2019, https://www.straitstimes.com/opinion/the-balance-between-national-progress-and-preservation-of-heritage.

IMAGE CREDITS

The author acknowledges the following for their assistance and kind permission to reproduce images in this book:

- Derek Heng and Kwa Chong Guan (Figure 4)
- Peter Borschberg (Figures 3 and 5)
- Marshall Cavendish (Figures 1 and 11)
- Ministry of Education and Star Publishing (Figure 9)
- National Library, Singapore (Figures 2, 7 and 8)
- Singapore Land Authority and National Archives of Singapore (Figure 6)

Index

About the Cover Illustrator

Caleb Tan is an illustrator from Singapore. He graduated from the School of Technology for the Arts, Republic Polytechnic, in 2009, and has been under the tutelage of experienced illustrators. He has worked with the Institute of Policy Studies, NUS on the published works of the IPS-Nathan Lecture Series. He was also the illustrator for Direct Life Foundation's *Where did Grandpa Go?* and *I Remember Grandma*. His illustrations usually feature whimsical narratives and lighthearted humour.